RECONSTRUCTING

VIBS

Volume 235

Robert Ginsberg
Founding Editor

Leonidas Donskis
Executive Editor

Associate Editors

G. John M. Abbarno
George Allan
Gerhold K. Becker
Raymond Angelo Belliotti
Kenneth A. Bryson
C. Stephen Byrum
Robert A. Delfino
Rem B. Edwards
Malcolm D. Evans
Roland Faber
Andrew Fitz-Gibbon
Francesc Forn i Argimon
Daniel B. Gallagher
William C. Gay
Dane R. Gordon
J. Everet Green
Heta Aleksandra Gylling
Matti Häyry
Brian G. Henning

Steven V. Hicks
Richard T. Hull
Michael Krausz
Olli Loukola
Mark Letteri
Vincent L. Luizzi
Adrianne McEvoy
J.D. Mininger
Peter A. Redpath
Arleen L. F. Salles
John R. Shook
Eddy Souffrant
Tuija Takala
Emil Višňovský
Anne Waters
James R. Watson
John R. Welch
Thomas Woods

a volume in
Philosophy and Psychology
PAP
Mark Letteri, Editor

RECONSTRUCTING SUBJECTS

A Philosophical Critique of Psychotherapy

Hakam H. Al-Shawi

Amsterdam - New York, NY 2011

Cover Photo: www.morguefile.com

Cover Design: Studio Pollmann

The paper on which this book is printed meets the requirements of "ISO 9706:1994, Information and documentation - Paper for documents - Requirements for permanence".

ISBN: 978-90-420-3404-4
E-Book ISBN: 978-94-012-0691-4
© Editions Rodopi B.V., Amsterdam - New York, NY 2011
Printed in the Netherlands

*To the many in the few
I dedicate this work*

CONTENTS

Editorial Foreword		ix
Acknowledgments		xi
Introduction		1
ONE	The Issue	5
	1. Insight-Oriented Psychotherapies	5
	2. Raising the Question	7
	3. Some Replies	10
TWO	Insight and Self-Knowledge	13
	1. The Issue	13
	2. The Self in Therapy	22
	3. Reconceptualizing Subjectivity and Self-Knowledge	36
THREE	Reconstruction and Absorption	45
	1. On Reconstruction	45
	2. On Absorption	47
	A. Suggestion	48
	B. Other Nonspecific Factors	51
	C. The Role of the Question	52
	D. Power-Interpretation	55
FOUR	Epistemological Issues	63
	1. Knowledge as Discovery	63
	2. Critique	69
	3. Knowledge as Construction	78
FIVE	Metaphysical Issues	87
	1. Two Versions of Realism	87
	2. Situated Realism	98
SIX	Ethical Considerations	113
	1. The Ethics of Insight-Oriented Psychotherapy	113
	2. Objections and Replies	116
Conclusion		121
Works Cited		125
About the Author		133
Index		135

EDITORIAL FOREWORD

I am pleased to present Hakam H. Al-Shawi's *Restructuring Subjects: A Philosophical Critique of Psychotherapy*, an incisive exploration of the most basic suppositions of psychotherapeutic practice. I first read Al-Shawi's manuscript as an interested colleague, not a reviewer, and I did not indicate that Editions Rodopi had recently appointed me to serve as a series editor. I questioned and re-questioned key elements of his project, and in every case he responded with seriousness and grace. Only after I interrogated thoroughly the vital lines of the project did I reveal the possibility of formal review and subsequent publication. Al-Shawi's work, then, is not just passionate but wholly conscientious, following the spirit of Nietzsche, the philosopher who places such a high value on honesty, and on whose perspective this project relies so manifestly. I cannot even say that I agree with all the principles and conclusions here. Philosophical inquiry is devoted, however, to a better understanding of the human condition, and heuristic and dialectical challenges are indispensable to the accomplishment of the task. Al-Shawi's arguments certainly provoke the reader to experience personal identity and transformation in new ways.

Mark Letteri
Philosophy and Psychology Series Editor

ACKNOWLEDGMENTS

The thoughts and ideas expressed in this work are the culmination of numerous hours and days spent reflecting on the material. Throughout that time, I was fortunate enough to benefit from valuable discussions and insightful commentary offered by many philosophers and friends. It is to them that I am deeply indebted to all that is good in this monograph. I would like to thank especially the editor of this series, Mark Letteri, for his patience and continued support throughout the years. Without his feedback on numerous earlier drafts, I am certain this project would not have been successfully completed. I am very grateful indeed and offer my sincere thanks.

Many individuals have influenced and shaped my thinking throughout the years I pondered and thought through the present material. In its infancy this project was inspired by two philosophers in particular: Andrew Brook and Béla Egyed. I am most grateful to them for my becoming! But the inspiration to become is not in itself enough to actualize a mature birth. Such a process requires an engagement with forces able to stimulate deeper thoughts and noble enough to trigger higher ones. I could not be more fortunate to have encountered such forces with Lorraine Code and David Jopling. I am indebted to them both for their unwavering support and assistance throughout the years.

There are countless other individuals to whom I am grateful for enduring me during the most turbulent times. In particular, I offer my gratitude to Cristian Berco for this journey that I am sure at times appeared insane to him. His unwavering support grounded me when I needed it most. I am also grateful to S. M. for her unconditional love and affirmation of my identities! To my mother and father, Hadia and Hisham, and to my sister, Manat, and my aunt, Majida, I offer my sincere thanks for their continued faith in me and for reinforcing my belief in what is possible. I could not have done it without you all.

Finally, I would like to acknowledge and thank Springer for publishing in volume 29 (2006) of *Human Studies* an earlier paper of mine, "Psychotherapy's Philosophical Values: Insight or Absorption?" which outlined some of the views in this monograph.

INTRODUCTION

[L]et me remind the reader that I am only an experimenter . . . . No facts are to me sacred; none are profane; I simply experiment, an endless seeker with no Past at my back. (Emerson, 1841/1903–1904, p. 318)

Many years ago, while in a philosophical conversation with a good friend of mine on the nature of emotions, he commented, "I must take responsibility for my emotions." But "why" I asked, curious for the philosophical reasoning behind his comment. To my great astonishment, he replied, "because my therapist told me so"! Of course, this incident perhaps tells me more about my friend than about psychotherapy, but over the years I have heard many such replies from various individuals, which always agitated me. And after reflecting on why such comments disturb me, the result is this study.

This study then, is about insight-oriented psychotherapies. It is also about much more than that. Along with Michel Foucault, who claimed that his objective was "to create a history of the different modes by which, in our culture, human beings are made subjects" (1983, p. 208), I would like to think that this study also is about the various forces in "civil" society that manufacture subjects and the values they espouse. And given the impact of insight-oriented psychotherapies upon millions of individuals, what better way is there to study how subjects are made? My interest in this study, however, is not in the detailed psychological theories and methodologies characterizing such therapies, but in the philosophical assumptions that underlie these practices. In the chapters that follow, my aim is to examine critically the epistemological and metaphysical foundations of insight-oriented psychotherapies in order to unveil the forces and mechanisms through which such therapies reconstruct subjects. By focusing on various philosophical concepts—principally those of subjectivity, knowledge, and reality—I bring to the foreground the hidden axiological dimensions constituting insight-oriented therapies and the world-view they maintain.

In parallel with my critical discussion, however, there is a constructive dimension which is an attempt to indicate a different way. While the critical aspect of this study may be characterized as a mapping of a problematic world-view, the constructive aspect is an indication towards a different way of thinking, being, and experiencing. Inspired by Friedrich Nietzsche, Gilles Deleuze, and Foucault, I attempt to outline a world-view in which traditional philosophical concepts, such as those of subjectivity, knowledge, and reality, may be understood differently. Driving and fueling my critical project then, is a desire to open a space for a different perspective: one that I believe is less repressive than its traditional counterpart. Whether I succeed in opening such a space, and in indicating a different direction, is for the reader to decide. However, it would be a mistake to interpret the constructive aspect of this study as being some social agenda for all to adopt. I do not believe this is possible. What I do hope for is a rupture in the certainty with which traditional philosophical concepts manifest themselves socially.

My approach to this critical/constructive study is guided by a Deleuzian understanding of philosophy which conceives of philosophy as "practice." For Deleuze, "philosophical theory is itself a practice, just as much as its object. It is no more abstract than its object. It is a practice of concepts, and it must be judged in the light of the other practices with which it interferes" (1989, p. 280). As a practice, philosophical theory for Deleuze is not the abstract study of some given object, but the "tracing" of concepts in various fields, unfolding their relation to other concepts and the terrain they map. This "tracing" indicates the possibility for creating new concepts and for establishing new lines of thought. As he comments, "[p]hilosophy is a constructivism, and constructivism has two qualitatively different complementary aspects: the creation of concepts and the laying out of a plane" (1994, pp. 35–36). As practice then, my approach in this study is to unfold those philosophical concepts operating in insight-oriented psychotherapies and to trace the concepts with which they are affiliated. More specifically, I approach the practice of concepts such as "subjectivity" and "knowledge" within insight-oriented psychotherapy and attempt to indicate how such practice is affiliated with the practice of concepts such as "absorption" and "reconstruction." Through such a tracing, I indicate other concepts which characterize a different world-view.

Such an approach, however, entails that this study is situated in the cracks between two philosophical traditions: the Anglo-American analytical tradition and the Continental schools of thought. In my belief in the value of both traditions, I attempt to present the following ideas in a manner that bespeaks both traditions. This is a difficult task, for on the one hand I wish to advance ideas and concepts in a clear and readily accessible way, while on the other I do not want the excessive demands of clarity and precision to prevent me from mapping concepts that do not easily render themselves accessible. This difficulty is especially apparent in the constructive dimension of this study, for I am attempting to present a different world-view employing traditional philosophical language and tools. Consequently, there is a tension running throughout this work that attempts to balance clarity and accessibility with senses that are not easily captured through language.

In chapter one, I begin by presenting the case of a fictional client who has undergone what might be considered a successful therapy. Assuming such a therapeutic outcome, and assuming that the client underwent some change during therapy, I raise several philosophical questions relating to the nature of this change. According to insight-oriented psychotherapy, our client's depressive and anxious state dramatically improved because of his newly found insights and the consequent self-knowledge gained. The therapy assisted him in discovering who he truly is, through the application of specific theories and methods. This raises the question of whether insight, self-knowledge, and self-discovery really do explain the change in the client.

To answer this question, I begin with an analysis of the concepts of self and insight as they are understood in insight-oriented psychotherapies, attempting to trace these concepts through a reading of Nietzsche and Immanuel Kant. This task is made exceedingly difficult by the lack of a clear philosophical conception of the self characterizing such therapies. Nevertheless, my analysis in this chapter suggests that insight-oriented psychotherapies assume an understanding of subjectivity similar to Kant's transcendental subject, and then proceed to reinforce this assumption through the psychotherapeutic process. Furthermore, I suggest that their assumption of such a subject and its associated world-view is ultimately based upon an inability to explicate a non-representational account of subjectivity and experience. What such an account would be like is the focus of the last section of the chapter.

In chapter three, I begin a tracing of concepts that are constitutive of psychotherapeutic practice as a dialogical encounter. This tracing suggests that contrary to what such therapies claim, the psychotherapeutic encounter reconstructs rather than discovers the client's self. Moreover, the reconstruction entails an "absorption" of the client into the therapist's philosophical framework that is characterized by certain conceptions of knowledge and reality. As it turns out, insight-oriented psychotherapy's claims to the discovery of self-knowledge are but a guise for the absorption of clients into a preconceived world-view. This conclusion entails that insight-oriented psychotherapy constitutes a deceptive set of practices.

Moreover, the philosophical framework or world-view clients are "absorbed" into is problematic, as chapters four and five indicate. In chapter four, I focus on the epistemological dimension of this world-view which is characterized by "S knows that p" claims. In its denial of the various forces constituting knowledge, and its reliance on representational knowledge, this epistemological stance proves to be extremely problematic. Indeed, I suggest that in its denial of real difference it indicates a certain epistemological fascism that is rooted in a valorization of concepts suggesting sameness and identity. Instead of such an epistemological stance, I suggest a conception of knowledge as construction where location and embodiment are taken into account as constitutive elements of knowledge production. This conception entails an understanding of knowledge as a production that remains always partial, incomplete, and in flux.

In chapter five, I consider metaphysical issues associated with the world-view clients are absorbed into. Focusing on versions of realism that may account for insight-oriented psychotherapy's metaphysical stance, I indicate the problematic nature of such realism and the questionable worldview it suggests. The implication of my analysis, however, is not a move to antirealism, but to another understanding of realism. This different understanding, which I characterize as "situated realism," suggests an altogether different world-view that I attempt to outline in the last section of the chapter.

I conclude this study with a brief but important examination, in chapter six, of some ethical issues relating to insight-oriented psychotherapies. I indicate that the ethical concerns with such therapies are quite substantial, since they involve a set of practices inevitably leading to a form of social control that serves to reinforce prevailing social norms. In the final section of the chapter, I consider some important objections and offer some replies.

One

THE ISSUE

1. Insight-Oriented Psychotherapies

Consider, for example, the report of a fictional client who believes his therapy was extremely successful in treating his depression and anxiety. Upon entering treatment, he was suffering from serious emotional and behavioral problems that had impacted his personal and professional life in various negative ways, dashing any hope for the future. Now, looking back and reflecting upon the course of his treatment, he judges it a complete success. He claims to be a *changed* person with a much better understanding of himself—his emotions, behaviors, and thoughts. He feels that he is now in touch with his *true* or *inner* self, which prior to therapy he was unable to apprehend. The therapeutic process gave him *insight* and *self-knowledge* that in turn allowed him to change for the better. And this was not just some intellectual understanding of himself, but a deeply felt experience, the kind "one feels . . . in one's bones" as Irvin Yalom would say (1989, p. 35). Sometimes, he maintains, the insights came suddenly, as if from nowhere, but mostly they surfaced through a gradual process of self-*discovery*. It has been a year now since he last saw his therapist, and his life has changed in innumerable positive ways. Not only has his personal and professional life improved, but his previous symptoms—the depression and anxiety—have virtually disappeared and he feels a new sense of self-confidence and hope for the future.

Depending on the particular theoretical orientation of his therapist, and assuming him to practice one or a combination of the insight-oriented psychotherapies, such as Freudian psychoanalysis, gestalt therapy, client-centered therapy, we may receive a number of differing theoretical accounts explaining this client's positive change and how his insight led to the outcome he reports. For example, had his therapist been a classical Freudian analyst, we would expect the therapist's report on the change this client experienced to be couched in classical psychoanalytic terms, relying on Freudian theory as an explicator. Most likely, the report would assess it as resulting from the application of a specific method of analysis—including free association and working through the transference—that sought to unveil those repressed unconscious forces that *caused* his troubles. By making conscious the previously unconscious, he was able to gain *insight* and *self-knowledge* that in turn allowed him to change. The analyst might consider himself an "archaeologist," assisting in the discovery of past causes that explain present effects. His task would be that "of reconstruction, resembl[ing] to a great extent an archaeologist's excavation of some dwelling-place that has been destroyed and buried or some ancient edifice" (Freud, 1937/1953-1974, p. 259).

Alternatively, our client might have seen a gestalt therapist who would provide a different theoretical explanation for his insight and change, including an altogether different process leading to it. He may explain the self-knowledge acquired as a result of the client's increased "awareness" of his "phenomenological field," bringing into the foreground of his perception what was "purposely and regularly relegated to the background" (Yontef and Jacobs, 2000, p. 314). Such increased "awareness" helps him to adapt and interact with his ever-changing environment, thus lessening the likelihood of neurosis (Perls, 1973, p. 25). As to methodology, the therapist would most likely have emphasized techniques that encouraged him to express his present feelings as a means of increasing his "awareness."

Of course, this client could also have seen any number of other insight-oriented therapists, whose reports would yet again differ from those just mentioned. He could have consulted a Jungian or Adlerian therapist, or one whose theoretical affiliations lean toward the newer schools of short-term psychodynamic therapy (Strupp and Bender, 1984), ego psychology (Blanck and Blanck, 1994), object relations (Greenberg and Mitchell, 1983), or self psychology (Kohut, 1971). Alternatively, he may have seen a client-centered therapist (Rogers, 1951) or an existential therapist (May, 1983; Yalom, 1980). And among all these schools further divisions proliferate depending upon the interpretations adopted. But, "[d]espite enormous theoretical and methodological differences . . . most of the insight-oriented psychotherapies agree on certain core principles" (Jopling, 2001, p. 21). They are:

> (1) Insight-oriented psychotherapy is a valid method of personal discovery that allows clients to discover truths about themselves, and to acquire bona fide self-knowledge; (2) the methods of the insight-oriented psychotherapies have specific and nonsuggestive effects; (3) one of the primary agents of therapeutic change in the insight-oriented psychotherapies is the therapist's use of interpretations; and (4) the client's acquisition of truth-tracking insight is a necessary condition for therapeutic improvement. (Jopling, 2001, p. 22)

Although individual insight-oriented psychotherapists may emphasize particular aspects of these principles, and would provide different theoretical explanations for therapeutic change, David Jopling's principles do characterize well those basic assumptions upon which differing theories and methodologies are built. Taken together, these principles constitute for Jopling what he entitles as "the standard view of insight-oriented psychotherapy" (p. 21). And since the purpose of this study is to consider the philosophical assumptions underlying insight-oriented psychotherapies, I will adopt this standard view only in so far as it represents the fundamental principles upon which such therapies rest. However, I do not wish to suggest that there is a "standard view" of insight-oriented psychotherapeutic theories, but only that certain fundamental principles are shared by the avowedly non-constructivist insight-oriented approaches to psychotherapy. While it may be the case that different insight-oriented psychotherapies place different emphases on theory and methodology, they concur in the belief that

> [i]t is through the process of self-awareness, self-understanding, and self-revelation that true growth occurs . . . . Their unifying dimension is the belief that insight into one's problems . . . is a necessary prerequisite before any real and lasting change can occur. (Kottler and Brown, 2000, p. 110)

2. Raising the Question

It would be surprising if the therapist did not consider our fictional client's change as validation of the specific psychotherapeutic theory and method applied. Typically for the therapist, the therapy clearly succeeded in alleviating this client's symptoms and in fostering a greater degree of self-knowledge. With reference to the standard view of insight-oriented psychotherapy, it might be said that the use of a specific method of therapy coupled with the therapist's correct interpretations induced in this client a process of self-discovery and insight that led to positive changes. Granting the client his claims that the therapy *changed* him and alleviated his symptoms, the question remains whether this change was truly due to self-discovery, self-knowledge, and insight brought about by the application of a specific insight-oriented psychotherapeutic theory and method coupled with a therapist's correct interpretations. Although change does seem to have occurred, we need not accept the standard view uncritically as an explanation for it.

Note, however, that I am not raising an empirical question here. I am not questioning whether any change occurred in the client, but whether the concepts employed by the standard view do provide an unproblematic explanation for this change. In other words, I wish to examine insight-oriented psychotherapy's conceptual understanding of insight and the self, and the epistemological-metaphysical assumptions that underlie the standard view. The standard view of psychotherapy, which supposedly serves as an explanation for the change occurring in therapy, relies on certain concepts. These include the concept of self, of insight, of knowledge, of discovery, of interpretation among others. And in relying on such concepts, insight-oriented psychotherapy must be assuming a certain understanding of them. The question I wish to address is whether such an understanding is problematic or not.

If, as I will claim in this study, insight-oriented psychotherapy's understanding of these concepts is problematic, then the standard view becomes a questionable explanation for the change occurring during psychotherapy. Moreover, if we are to understand these concepts differently from the way insight-oriented psychotherapy understands them, and if we are to examine those elements which constitute any psychotherapeutic relationship, what does this tell us about the nature of the change occurring in such therapies?

Consider the concepts of insight and the self. According to the standard view, insight-oriented psychotherapy is a method which "allows clients to discover truths about themselves, and to acquire bona fide self-knowledge." This, in turn, assists in therapeutic improvement, a necessary condition of which is "the client's acquisition of truth-tracking insight." Put differently, through the attainment of insight into the nature of the self, and through personal discovery and the acquisition of self-knowledge, clients improve. The concepts of insight and the self are therefore pivotal in insight-oriented psychotherapy. But, one may ask, as I do in this study, what is the operative understanding of these concepts within insight-oriented psychotherapy, and is it unproblematic? If their understanding of these concepts is questionable, how should we then understand insight and the self? In chapter two, I address these questions claiming that insight-oriented psychotherapy's understanding of insight, the self, and self-knowledge is problematic. Consequently, I suggest a different understanding of these concepts.

But if insight-oriented psychotherapy's understanding of such crucial concepts as those of insight and the self is questionable, and if insight and the self are conceptualized in an altogether different way, what is the nature of this change that does occur during psychotherapy? As I will claim in chapters two and three, contrary to what is claimed by insight-oriented psychotherapies, clients do not necessarily discover certain aspects of their true selves, hence gaining greater self-knowledge during the course of therapy. In fact, the very reference to a "true self" is itself problematic, suggesting that no such self is discovered during therapy. On the contrary, as I will claim, a certain conception of a discoverable self is assumed at the very outset of therapy, which is then supported and reinforced by the psychotherapeutic process. Consequently, a self is not discovered in therapy, but constructed through certain mechanisms constitutive of the psychotherapeutic process.

The change that does occur in insight-oriented psychotherapy, then, raises some very crucial conceptual questions which, in turn, suggest other concepts to explain the change. These include the concepts of (re)construction and absorption, as I will claim in chapter three. Again, however, this should not be construed as an empirical dispute, resolvable through some kind of empirical observation. My focus and interest in this study is philosophical, seeking to unravel and understand certain key concepts which constitute the dialogical encounter that is insight-oriented psychotherapy.

My claim is that reconstruction and absorption constitute the encounter, and that these concepts undermine the claims put forth by the standard view. As such, it is not a question of empirically observing the psychotherapeutic encounter, but of conceptually analyzing elements intrinsic to insight-oriented psychotherapy as a dialogical encounter.

But the philosophical issues and concerns are even greater. The standard view of insight-oriented psychotherapy is situated within a certain understanding of knowledge that we need not accept uncritically. And since such an understanding plays a crucial role within the psychotherapeutic process, we need to question it and examine it in order to ascertain its acceptability. This raises several questions. First, what is insight-oriented psychotherapy's understanding of knowledge? Second, is it problematic? Third, if it is problematic, how are we to understand knowledge? As I will claim in chapter four, insight-oriented psychotherapy assumes an extremely problematic conception of knowledge as "discovery." Alternatively, I will suggest a conception of knowledge based on construction, and a situated and positioned knower.

Since epistemological stances assume a certain metaphysical stance, the issues pertaining to the nature of knowledge as understood by insight-oriented psychotherapies invite a questioning of the metaphysical assumptions underlying such therapies. In other words, we also need not accept uncritically the metaphysical assumptions made by insight-oriented therapies. This metaphysical questioning invites questions relating to "realism" and "antirealism," asking for possible metaphysical accounts to situate the standard view, and asking whether such accounts are problematic. And, as I will claim in chapter five, the varieties of "realism" that may account for the standard view are highly suspect. This claim, however, does not necessarily imply a move to "antirealism," but an unfolding of another understanding of "realism" which I call "situated realism."

Questioning the change that occurs in insight-oriented psychotherapy then, invites an analysis of several key concepts. These concepts, I believe, form the corner stone of insight-oriented psychotherapy, and are crucial components, defining it as a certain psychotherapeutic practice. But such questioning also invites ethical concerns. If, as I have indicated already, insight-oriented psychotherapy is founded upon a philosophically questionable understanding of key concepts, then the standard view, as an explanation for the client's therapeutic change, is problematic. If this is so, then is the client being deceived in some way? Presumably, at the end of a successful psychotherapeutic encounter, clients emerge from therapy believing to have discovered some "truths" about themselves, and attained greater insight into their "true" self. Alternatively, they may emerge from therapy having acquired at least certain useful tools and reflective habits that presumably would lead to the discovery of certain "truths" about themselves. For our fictional client, he feels that now he is in touch with his true or inner self, which prior to therapy he was unable to apprehend. The psychotherapeutic process assisted him in gaining insight and self-knowledge that in turn allowed him to change for the better. But if the standard view is problematic, then is our fictional client being deceived? Did the psychotherapeutic process deceive him into believing in such so-called discoveries? This will be the main focus of chapter six, where I will claim deception is at the very heart of the psychotherapeutic encounter.

3. Some Replies

The standard view's explanation for the change occurring in insight-oriented psychotherapy has not gone unchallenged. One response that takes issue with the standard view's explanation revolves around certain factors common to all psychotherapies that contribute to therapeutic change (Frank, 1989; Calestro, 1972; Strupp, 1972). These factors, which are not specific to any particular psychotherapeutic theory or methodology, contribute in varying degrees to the outcome of therapy. As Jerome Frank indicates, at least four components are identifiable (1989, pp. 100–101). First, all therapies involve an emotional relationship with a therapist who is recognized as a knowledgeable and authoritative figure willing to listen and help. Second, all therapies involve a setting that situates the client in an atmosphere considered both safe and indicative of the therapist's authoritative position as the healer. Third, they present some explanation for the client's symptoms and a procedure for alleviating them. And fourth, all therapies require both the therapist and client to participate in a process believed by both as beneficial.

While different insight-oriented therapies may exhibit these components in varying degrees, they all endorse them, at least minimally. This commonality, in turn, brings into question the standard view's explanation for what is occurring in the therapy by drastically reducing the significance of insight and the role of any specific theory and methodology (Jopling, 2008, pp. 82–83). If, irrespective of insight or the particular theory and method applied, these components contribute significantly to therapeutic change in insight-oriented therapies, then the standard view's claims for the significance of insight gained through the application of a particular theory and method lose credence. That is, the specificity of any particular theory and method would not be as important for therapeutic change, since more general factors may account for the change. However, as Jopling indicates, this does not imply that neither insight nor a specific theory and method is needed (pp. 85–86). While it may be true that any type of insight-oriented therapy would produce therapeutic change, some specific theory and method operating throughout the therapy remains necessary if only to allow for the operation of these components. Since these components are general in nature, in order for them to operate, it may be necessary to situate them within the confines of a psychotherapeutic setting that professes a specific theory and method. For example, consider the first component identified by Frank. If all therapies involve an emotional relationship with a therapist who is recognized as a knowledgeable and authoritative figure willing to listen and help, then a psychotherapeutic situation recognizing the therapist as such may be required in order to allow for the operation of this factor. And it would be difficult to have such a psychotherapeutic situation without some specific theory and method to justify it.

The conceptual issues however, that I identify in the previous section, remain, for the components I have listed only provide us with an answer to how therapeutic change is occurring. According to the standard view, how therapeutic change occurs depends primarily on insight, self-knowledge, and the application of a specific theory and method. But according to Frank's components, this is not entirely the case since other factors—namely, his components—describe how such a change occurs. Indeed, according to the third factor, that a client be given an explanation for her or his symptoms, it is possible for the explanation to be both fictitious and yet therapeutically beneficial nonetheless. But the conceptual issues revolving around the nature of insight and self-knowledge remain, for Frank's components suggest only that their role in therapeutic change is diminished. They do not explain the role of what is diminished. Once an analysis of insight and self-knowledge is undertaken, as I propose to do in this study, it becomes evident why these concepts, as understood by insight-oriented psychotherapies, are problematic explicators for therapeutic change. As such, Frank's four components do not preclude the analysis I wish to undertake, for the meanings of insight, self-knowledge, self-understanding, remain unclear and are not at all self-evident. Although there is much reference to these concepts in the psychotherapeutic literature, critical analysis remains largely absent—a somewhat surprising development since they underlie insight-oriented therapies and are central to clinical practice.

Jopling, in his 2001 paper "Placebo Insight: The Rationality of Insight-Oriented Psychotherapy," offers a different challenge to the standard view's explanation for therapeutic change. By arguing that pseudo-insights or placebo insights are just as likely, if not more likely, to generate therapeutic change, Jopling undermines the fundamental belief that therapeutic change results only from genuine—that is truthful—insight and self-knowledge. The epistemic pressures upon the client in such forms of therapy, such as incorrect interpretations, result in making the therapeutic encounter "likely to generate illusions, deceptions, pseudo-insights, and adaptive self-misunderstandings that convincingly mimic bona fide insight" (Jopling, 2001, p. 25). Moreover, this consequence is not due to "failures in the application of the treatment methods but failures in the methods and the therapeutic theories themselves" (p. 25). This fact, however, does not imply that no epistemic conditions would allow for genuine insight, but that the general model's assumptions cannot be accepted as the only explanation for therapeutic change (p. 32). Indeed, in *Self-Knowledge and the Self*, Jopling (2000) provides a discussion of the requirements for the possibility of self-knowledge.

Even if we agree with Jopling that pseudo-insights or placebo insights may explain therapeutic change, it remains to be seen what would constitute "genuine" insight and whether insight-oriented psychotherapy's understanding of this concept is unproblematic. As I will argue, insight is a questionable concept in insight-oriented psychotherapies because of its reliance on a suspect conception of the self. Consequently, insight-oriented psychotherapies cannot adequately explain therapeutic change in terms of insight. Moreover, the "realist" metaphysic or world-view—terms I consider in chapter five—implicit in Jopling's distinction between genuine and pseudo-insights requires critical examination, for only within the frame of such a metaphysic can one distinguish between genuine and pseudo-insights. However, as I will argue, the "realist" metaphysic of insight-oriented therapies is itself problematic and cannot be accepted uncritically.

Jopling's and Frank's critiques constitute important and significant contributions to explaining the change occurring in insight-oriented psychotherapies. They indicate why the standard view's assumptions cannot be accepted uncritically. However, I do not believe they go far enough in their critiques, for their positions only partially explain the change a client undergoes during therapy. As this study will show, the change which occurs in such therapies is not due to any self-knowledge, insight, or self-understanding because the manner in which insight-oriented psychotherapy understands these notions is extremely suspect. Alternatively, I will suggest that clients are reconstructed during the course of therapy and subsequently drawn into the therapist's philosophical framework, which is characterized by problematic epistemological and metaphysical assumptions. Although subsequent chapters will expand and defend these claims more fully, suffice it to say at this stage that certain mechanisms, such as suggestion, contribute to "absorbing" clients into a philosophical world-view that poses as the "discovery" of the client's psychological state. Not only does this process serve to reinforce socially accepted values, as I claim in chapter six, but it is deceptive; deceiving clients into believing they have gained genuine insight into their true selves. This deception raises some very serious ethical concerns which I discuss in chapter six.

Two

INSIGHT AND SELF-KNOWLEDGE

1. The Issue

Insight—that fulfilling goal of those who seek self-knowledge and self-understanding—constitutes a central hallmark, a defining objective of therapies aiming at excavating the psyche. Insight's reputed critical role in fostering client autonomy and agency and in enlightening previously confused and disillusioned clients marks it as a requirement for therapeutic improvement (Jopling, 2008, pp. 48–54). Moreover, it serves as a means of validating the specific therapeutic modality being applied (pp. 78–79). Yet, despite its widespread significance, little agreement exists on what constitutes insight in therapy. Depending upon the particular therapeutic modality—indeed, on the particular therapist—the nature and content of insight varies dramatically, making it difficult to formulate a generic definition of the concept in insight-oriented psychotherapies.

Borrowing and adapting an account from Irvin Yalom that is meant as an example of how existential therapy is more successful than the psychoanalytic approach in addressing compulsive sexual behavior, consider once again our fictional client and his claim that insight and the consequent self-knowledge gained allowed him to change for the better (Yalom, 1980, pp. 191–194). During the course of therapy, he revealed he had had numerous sexual relationships with men, perhaps in the hundreds, and to none of them had he felt any emotional ties. For him, these men were simply "things" to be used as objects for sexual gratification and, as such, were "more or less interchangeable." Often, he found himself in pursuit of yet another man only moments after discarding the previous one, for he had this "need," this "craving," for a hunt even though he really did not want to undertake it.

Depending upon the particular theoretical orientation of his therapist, the insights explaining his behavior would very likely differ. As I explain in the following chapter, this is probably due to the various factors influencing him during therapy. For example, had he been to a Freudian analyst, we would not be surprised to hear him offer an account that might run as follows: "I discovered that I had unresolved issues with my parents. This explained my desire for, but fear of, men who resembled my father, and showed why the closer I got in my travels to the city where my father lived, the stronger was my sexual desire. Also, it explained to me the various incestuous dreams that haunted me for a long period. Furthermore, I discovered that my compulsive homosexuality was driven by a need to handle unconscious heterosexual impulses." Yet, had he seen an existential psychotherapist, his insights would likely be explained differently. His account might now be: "I discovered that my compulsive sexual appetite was driven by a fear of being alone, which made me very anxious and which drove me to seek the company of other men. In time, however, I realized that my anxiety was really death anxiety, and sex was a means for me to overcome this fear. It made me feel alive and in contact with life. I needed to be in the constant company of men so that I would not be alone, and have to confront the possibility of death. Although I still have some death anxiety, I feel much more in control of my life nowadays, and am able to abstain from sexual relations. I realize that when the opportunity presents itself, I am free to choose." And, depending on the theoretical orientation of his therapist, any number of other accounts is possible.

Despite such differences in the nature and content of insight, David Jopling has identified some common elements of the concept within insight-oriented psychotherapies that broadly capture insight "as the condition that occurs when clients acquire an emotionally charged and action-guiding understanding" of

> (1) the kinds of disorders from which they are suffering, and the symptoms with which the disorders are associated; (2) the causes and/or meanings of their disorders; (3) the relation between the causes and/or meanings of their disorders, and their overall life processes, including their behaviors, emotions, and personality. (2008, p. 68)

Once these conditions have been met, a further condition stipulates that insight occurs when:

> (4) clients *believe* that their understanding of (1)–(3) is valid, and when they *believe* that the validity of their understanding is measured against and confirmed by the relevant psychological, behavioral, and historical facts. (p. 68)

Of course, what is considered as a disorder may itself depend upon the theoretical orientation of the psychotherapist. That is, depending upon the particular type of therapy enlisted, a certain behavior may or may not be considered a disorder.

Combined with the fundamental principles of insight-oriented psychotherapies I have presented in chapter one under the standard view, these conditions for insight suggest a psychotherapeutic process whereby clients "discover" or "get in touch with," a "real," "inner," "core," or "authentic" self (Jopling, 2008, p. 11). Although the psychotherapeutic process is thought to assist in the discovery of such a preexisting self, the claim is that it does not fabricate it, but only allows what was previously hidden to surface. The acquisition of such truthful self-knowledge is one of the key factors contributing to therapeutic change which results in the alleviation of symptoms.

Accordingly, insight, as defined by insight-oriented psychotherapies, constitutes the acquisition of veridical self-knowledge, which includes knowledge of the client's psychological and emotional make-up, personality structure, behaviors and dispositions. Such self-knowledge is founded upon the assumption that there is a "real" or "core" diachronic self, an "I" existing through time, discoverable through the application of a specific theory and method. By unveiling the causes and/or meanings of disorders, and establishing a relation between such causes and/or meanings and the client's overall life processes, knowledge of the real nature of the self is gained. As such, the answer to the question "Who am I?" lies in discovering my past: in discovering those hidden causes and/or meanings that have shaped my behaviors, emotions, and personality.

For insight-oriented psychotherapies, insight provides a means to self-knowledge through a *backward* looking process which attempts to trace the life history of a subject through the *discovery* of causes and/or meanings and their relations to behaviors, emotions, and personality. Although the degree of emphasis placed on the past depends upon the particular theoretical orientation, its role is critical in most insight-oriented psychotherapies. Stated otherwise, in order for me to understand who I am and to gain insight and self-knowledge, I need to journey into my past with the assistance of a professional travel guide, so that I may discover those relations that have constituted me. Although the hope is that such newly gained insight and self-knowledge will better shape the client's future, the degree to which future behaviors, emotions, and personality are modified depends on the degree of insight and self-knowledge gained as discovery of the "real" self.

But is such an understanding of insight and consequent self-knowledge possible within the confines of insight-oriented psychotherapies? Is there some "true," "core," or "real" self existing through time from the moment of its inception to its death? Or, is such an understanding of subjectivity based upon an assumption derived from a certain world-view and a certain understanding of experience that assumes the existence of such a self? In other words, is it possible that certain historical forces or factors, assuming a certain world-view, have led to such an understanding of the self? Moreover, why does self-knowledge require at least a minimal journey into the past? These are the questions that will occupy the remainder of this chapter. As I will show, insight and self-knowledge as defined by insight-oriented psychotherapies raise some serious concerns and indeed cannot be realized within such therapies.

Before proceeding further however, it is important to detour briefly into a consideration of various examples within psychotherapeutic literature that indicate insight terminology, and to note some of the epistemological criticisms and responses such terminology has invited particularly with respect to psychoanalysis. Focusing initially on various examples of insight terminology, it should be noted that it is difficult to find many psychotherapeutic schools—with the exception of the behavioral therapies—that would *deny* the role of insight as a tool for therapeutic change. As Willard Gaylin maintains in *Talk is Not Enough: How Psychotherapy Really Works*: "[I]nsight is a useful, perhaps necessary, ingredient for change. Whatever it may be called—self-knowledge, self-awareness, insight—it is still central to most schools of psychotherapy" (2000, p. 147). Moreover, such insight does not necessarily have to occur during the psychotherapeutic session. In client-centered therapy, for example, Carl Rogers maintains that often "the significant insights occur between interviews" and while appearing simple, they come "to have emotional and operational *meaning*," which give them their "newness and vividness" (1951, p. 119).

Within the psychodynamic psychotherapies, the role of insight is perhaps even more significant than in other forms of insight-oriented psychotherapy. Indeed, according to John Frosch in *Psychodynamic Psychiatry: Theory and Practice*, insight "is supposed to be the essence of psychoanalytic theory, or other exploratory psychotherapies" (1990, p. 720). Also, as Michael Jacobs comments in *Psychodynamic Counselling in Action*:

> To make good use of the psychodynamic approach, the client needs to show some insight (understanding) of her or himself, and also to respond thoughtfully (although not compliantly) to linking responses and interpretations. (1999, p. 44)

However, the psychotherapeutic literature is not at all clear on what this insight is supposed to mean, except that it involves the discovery of some determinate psychic reality—a reality that includes, for example, emotions, wishes, desires, fantasies, memories, patterns of interpersonal relating, defenses and resistances. In Frosch, for example, insight operates at many levels through a kind of feedback mechanism that prepares the patient for the acquisition of deeper and deeper insights. As he maintains:

> The achieving of insight and the effect of acquiring insight as a therapeutic phenomenon is a reciprocal, and almost a feedback mechanism. For example, we cannot make certain interpretations until the patient is ready. This means that a great deal more must go on in a patient before he is able to see the connections. If he is ready, then the seeing of connections will be meaningful and helpful. This being made ready is a complex procedure consisting of many phenomena, among which are even preliminary insight experiences. I would therefore say that insight is the acquiring by the patient of an understanding of connections and

relations. That this may take place at many levels, and is an integral part of the reciprocal manner in which the deeper forms of psychotherapy develop. (1990, p. 720)

But, we may ask, what is it that makes a patient "ready" to acquire "deeper" insights? Could it be, as I will suggest in the next chapter that being ready implies the absorption of the patient into the therapist's framework?

Another explanation for insight is provided by Stanley Messer and C. Seth Warren in their *Models of Brief Psychodynamic Therapy*, where they clearly imply that through the discovery of one's character traits, wishes, and needs, greater self-understanding is attained, which consequently leads to change. According to them:

> The simplest and most frequent answer given to the question of what brings about change is the patient's acquisition of insight, aided largely by the therapist's interventions, especially their interpretations and clarifications. The expansion of patients' self-understanding and awareness allows them to break out of their neurotic mode, to resolve their conflicts, and to resume growth and maturation . . . by becoming more fully aware of one's defences, wishes, needs, resistances, character traits, and conflicts, one is in a much better position to exercise control over them. Otherwise, they continue to exert an insidious influence beyond one's ken or control. If one has been anxious, inhibited, unproductive, or depressed, the route to overcome such dysfunctional states, according to psychoanalytic theory, is by becoming conscious of the conflicts underlying these symptoms. (1995, p. 93)

Coupled with what Glen Gabbard maintains in *Psychodynamic Psychiatry in Clinical Practice: The DSM-IV Edition*, a certain view within the psychotherapeutic literature emerges. According to Gabbard,

> [t]he ultimate goals of psychoanalysis and those treatments weighted toward the expressive end of the continuum involve the acquisition of insight, which may be defined as the capacity to understand the unconscious meanings and origins of one's symptoms and behavior. (1994, p. 91)

What emerges is the suggestion that the psychotherapeutic process is one whereby clients "discover" or "get in touch with" some determinate and preexisting psychic reality. The assumption is that this reality constitutes who they really are as individuals. This view is even more apparent if we shift our focus to psychoanalysis in particular.

Consider, for example, the Freudian analyst Robert Waelder and his description of a successful analysis.

> In a successful analysis, the patient eventually becomes aware of the previously unconscious elements in his neurosis: he can fully feel and experience how his neurotic symptoms grew out of the conflict of which he is now conscious; and he can fully feel and experience how facing up to these conflicts dispels the symptoms and, as Freud put it, "transform neurotic suffering into everyday misery"; and how flinching will bring the symptoms back again. (1962, p. 629)

This account clearly demonstrates how the psychoanalytic process is an unfolding or an unraveling of what was previously hidden or concealed within the patient's unconscious. By making conscious what was previously unconscious, the neurotic suffering is transformed. This process of discovering the patient's "real" or "true" psychic constitution is based on Sigmund Freud's belief in the developmental origins of psychological problems. As Michael Basch explains in *Doing Psychotherapy*,

> "[i]nsight," "psychoanalytically oriented" or "depth" psychotherapy . . . is based on Freud's recognition that psychological problems are developmental, and that only by obtaining insight into the process that gives rise to them can a resolution based on cause be reached. (1980, p. 171)

For Freud, psychoanalysis provided the necessary key to unlock the unconscious successfully and subsequently cure the patient. This process entailed the discovery of a determinate psychic reality through the use of correct or truthful interpretations. Commenting on the case history of Little Hans, Freud maintained that although some patients may require more assistance than others,

> there are none who get through without some of it. Slight disorders may perhaps be brought to an end by the subject's unaided efforts, but never a neurosis . . . . To get the better of such an element another person must be brought in, and in so far as that other person can be of assistance the neurosis will be curable. (1909/1953–1974, p. 104)

And to cure the neurosis, the interpretations offered by the analyst and accepted by the patient had to be truthful in such a way that they corresponded with what was real in the patient. "After all, his conflicts will only be successfully solved and his resistances overcome if the anticipatory ideas he is given tally with what is real in him" (Freud, 1917/1953–1974, p. 452). If they do not tally, then they need to be replaced "by something more correct" (p. 452).

The epistemological problem of whether Freud's patients were merely talked into accepting fanciful but psychologically and historically false interpretations—and the related problem of whether psychoanalysis is a sophisticated form of suggestion therapy—was first raised by Freud's colleague Wilhelm Fliess. It was later taken up by several generations of philosophers and psychologists concerned with the scientific status of psychoanalysis, and the nature of clinical evidence: for example, Ludwig Wittgenstein, John Wisdom, Brian Farrell, Paul Ricoeur, Adolf Grünbaum, Edward Erwin, Donald Spence, Richard Rorty, and Roy Schafer.

Drawing from Freud's claims on the necessity of the psychoanalytic process to cure neuroses, and for interpretations' need to tally with what is real in the patient, Grünbaum has characterized Freud's remarks as the Tally Argument. According to Grünbaum (1984, pp. 139–140), Freud's Tally Argument consists of two premises and two conclusions.

> Premise 1: [O]nly the psychoanalytic method of interpretation and treatment can yield or mediate to the patient correct insight into the unconscious pathogens of his psychoneurosis.
> Premise 2: [T]he analysand's correct insight into the etiology of his affliction and into the unconscious dynamics of his character is, in turn, *causally necessary* for the therapeutic conquest of his neurosis.

Coupled with Freud's claims on the existence of patients P who have been through psychoanalysis successfully, these two premises yield two conclusions.

> Conclusion 1: The psychoanalytic interpretations of the hidden causes of P's behavior given to him by his analyst are indeed correct, and thus—as Freud put it—these interpretations "tally with what is real" in P.
> Conclusion 2: Only analytic treatment could have wrought the conquest of P's psychoneurosis.

For Grünbaum, Freud's Tally Argument is a tool for Freud to maintain the crucial epistemological position that "actual *durable* therapeutic success guarantees *not only* that the pertinent analytic interpretations *ring* true or credible to the analysand *but also* that they *are* indeed veridical, or at least quite close to the mark" (Grünbaum, 1984, p. 140).

The Tally Argument, however, is hardly acceptable according to Grünbaum who questions it on various grounds that individually and collectively seriously undermine Freud's claims (Grünbaum, 1984, 1993). Moreover, not only are the Tally Argument's two premises highly questionable, but no empirical alternative seems available (Grünbaum, 1984, p. 166). Although it is beyond the scope of this study to go into the intricate details of Grünbaum's arguments, it is important to note that his critique of Freud ranges across many issues that include the role of suggestion, doctrinal compliance, introspective accuracy, placebo effects, and spontaneous remission in analysis. With respect to suggestion for example, which I consider in greater detail in the following chapter, Grünbaum argues that it "is at once the decisive agent in his [Freud's] therapy, and the cognitive bane of the psychoanalytic method of investigation" (1984, p. 160). Contrary to Freud's claims as reflected in the Tally Argument, Grünbaum argues that psychoanalysis amounts to a form of suggestion therapy that has little bearing on the historical and psychological truth, and is based on spurious and suggestion-contaminated clinical data that results in pseudo-confirmations of its main theoretical claims. Freud, of course, was well aware of the threat posed by suggestion and the charges it brought against his claims for veridical insight (Freud, 1917/1953–1974, pp. 446–447). Indeed, according to Grünbaum, the Tally Argument was meant to overcome such charges, and to vindicate Freud's epistemological claims. However, according to Grünbaum,

> evidence accumulating in the most recent decades [from, for example, outcome studies of psychotherapeutic treatment, and research in cognitive psychology on introspection and causal self-attribution] makes . . . the Tally Argument well-nigh empirically untenable, and thus devastatingly undermines the conclusions that Freud drew from it. (1984, p. 128)

Later in his career, Freud recognized the weakness of the Tally Argument, and allowed that the therapeutic effectiveness of interpretations may stem not from their psychological and historical truth, but from the patient's *conviction* in their truth.

Such charges against psychoanalysis have prompted various responses that aim at rescuing it from being a mere suggestion-based form of therapy. One such response is provided by Spence (1982) who claims that epistemological critiques of the evidentiary base and scientific status of Freudian psychoanalysis rest on a confusion between narrative and historical truth (p. 27). This confusion is due in part to Freud's archaeological metaphor, which suggests that historical truth is the key to a successful psychoanalytic encounter. Spence argues that it is vital to distinguish between the two kinds of truth.

> Narrative truth can be defined as the criterion we use to decide when a certain experience has been captured to our satisfaction; it depends on continuity and closure and the extent to which the fit of the pieces takes

> on an aesthetic finality. Narrative truth is what we have in mind when we say that such and such is a good story, that a given explanation carries conviction, that *one* solution to a mystery must be true. Once a given construction has acquired narrative truth, it becomes just as real as any other kind of truth; this new reality becomes a significant part of the psychoanalytic cure. (Spence, 1982, p. 31)

Crucially, the truth of an analyst's interpretation, the patient's insight, or the clinical case history, does not depend on a correspondence with actual events, but on the coherence, plausibility, and internal consistency of the narrative. This understanding of truth is to be contrasted with historical truth.

> Historical truth is time-bound and is dedicated to the strict observance of correspondence rules; our aim is to come as close as possible to what "really" happened. Historical truth is not satisfied with coherence for its own sake; we must have some assurance that the pieces being fitted into the puzzle also belong to a certain time and place and that this belonging can be corroborated in some systematic manner. (Spence, 1982, p. 32)

Unfortunately, much of what Freud wrote reflects historical truth, but if we are to focus on what he did—that is, on how he wrote, interpreted, and assembled his explanations—we see the operation of narrative truth (Spence, 1982, p. 32). Indeed, it is the coherence and fit of the narrative in psychoanalysis that mistakenly makes us believe we are dealing with historical truth (p. 27). This confusion is understandable since narrative truth has a reality and an immediacy that "carries an important significance for the process of therapeutic change" (p. 21). For Spence then, the route out of the epistemological criticisms leveled against Freudian psychoanalysis rests on a recognition that psychoanalytic interpretations, and by implication patients' insights, are a construction rather than a reconstruction "that is supposed to correspond to something in the past" (p. 35). In other words, psychoanalytic interpretations depend upon narrative truth rather than on an historical correspondence with past events. And such constructive interpretations are able to bring about a positive change in the patient because they appear "to relate the known to the unknown, to provide explanation in place of uncertainty" (p. 290).

This recognition of interpretations as creative constructions rather than reconstructions allows Spence to respond directly to Grünbaum's challenges. Since interpretations do not necessarily have to tally with actual past events in order to be therapeutically effective, the Tally Argument "is something of a straw man" (p. 290). As Spence states, "interpretations may be effective without necessarily being 'true' in a strict historical sense" (p. 290). As such,

Grünbaum's challenges lose much of their force in attempting to undermine Freudian psychoanalysis.

Other philosophers and psychologists have tried different strategies to protect the credibility of psychoanalytic interpretations from charges of suggestion, and to protect psychoanalysis from the charge of pseudo-science. It has been claimed, for example, that psychoanalytic interpretations and the insights they lead to are merely useful tools or heuristic devices that may point to the truth (Wisdom, 1969); that they are more like texts than scientific records of psychological fact (Ricoeur, 1970, 1977); or that they are useful vocabularies for coping with the problems of life, and that the very idea of psychological truth is incoherent (Rorty, 1986).

Yet another response from the narrative-hermeneutic school comes from Schafer (1976), who has argued for a metaphoric interpretation of Freud's metapsychology rather than a literal reading of such notions as discharges, energy, and cathexes. This is because, for Schafer, "[w]hat is in question is not the findings of psychoanalysis; it is the best language in which to render them and systematize them" (1976, p. X). In other words, what is problematic in Freudian psychoanalysis is the language used. This move, which in some respects is similar to Spence's in that they both focus on a confusion in reading Freud, prompts Schafer to propose a new language for psychoanalysis that is an action language.

> One shall regard every psychological process, event, experience, response, or other item of behavior as an action, and one shall designate it by an active verb and, when appropriate and useful, by an adverb or an adverbial locution that states the mode of this action. (Schafer, 1976, pp. 363–364)

Through a focus on "actions," which include "all private psychological activity that can be made public" (p. 9), Schafer hopes to overcome the various criticisms leveled against Freud which, according to Schafer, are a result of Freud's language.

Although psychoanalysis is not the focus of this study, the various epistemological critiques brought against it, and the responses such critiques have generated, are important reminders of the seriousness and complexity of the issues surrounding claims to insight. Moreover, they indicate a long tradition in which claims to insight have been questioned: a tradition which perhaps goes back at least to the Presocratics.

2. The Self in Therapy

Commenting on the influence of postmodern theory in therapy, Barbara Held maintains that despite postmodern claims to a "fragmented, ephemeral, inconsistent, fluid, fluctuating" conception of the self, postmodern therapists must still assume a certain ontological sense of the subject/individual in their practice (1995, pp. 16–19). While it is not clear what an ontological sense of the subject/individual is supposed to mean, the general idea seems to indicate the positing of some thing, substance, or entity continuing through time. "There is, it seems, no way around the need to take seriously the notion of the individual, at least when one does or speaks about psychotherapy" (p. 19). For Held, psychotherapy must assume some ontological sense of the self/individual/subject continuing through time because even postmodern psychotherapists who desire to individualize each client, considering each one a specific and uniquely situated individual, must assume the existence of such an individual in the first place. But, I do not see how this must imply that postmodern psychotherapy must assume an ontological sense of the subject, since it remains possible that postmodern psychotherapists have misunderstood or misapplied postmodern theory to psychotherapy! That is, in their desire to apply postmodern theory to psychotherapy, postmodern therapists might have (mis)interpreted postmodern conceptions of the self in such a way so as to allow for psychotherapeutic practice. Alternatively, it may be that non-postmodern psychotherapists have failed to recognize the radically different metaphysical stance or world-view in which postmodern psychotherapists situate themselves and the concepts they employ.

But there is also an ethical issue at stake for Held. According to her, conceptualizing the self as fragmented or decentered "is certainly no ideal of mental health . . . to which any serious practicing clinician, *modern or postmodern*, would in all good conscience subscribe" (p. 19). While it is not very clear to me why Held maintains this, presumably it is because subscribing to such a postmodern conception of the self entails a rejection of an individual's uniqueness in therapy which "reflects something enduring to his self/identity as it really exists" (p. 20). But why should the ideals of mental health include recognition of an individual's uniqueness in therapy? Why not maintain a fragmented and decentered self as an ideal of mental health? As I will claim in chapter five, ethical decisions depend to a very large extent on the question of value, and on what is being valued. As such, we need not accept as unethical a fragmented and decentered conception of the self.

The key point at this stage, however, is that the assumption of a self or individual continuing through time in an ontological sense constitutes a founding principle of psychotherapy, and is not restricted to insight-oriented therapies. Furthermore, as Held suggests, a rejection of this assumption seems to imply serious ethical consequences regarding good practice and the pursuit of mental health. With the majority of insight-oriented psychotherapies, in particular, not only is an ontological commitment about the concept of self assumed, but also that some degree of a backward looking process is necessary to unveiling what was previously inaccessible to the client. And as

I will indicate shortly, this need to journey into the past raises some concerns.

It is surprising then, given the centrality of the concept of self within insight-oriented psychotherapy, that there is no clear and consistent account of what the concept is supposed to mean. While there is an ontological commitment to the concept indicating the existence of some discoverable self, accounts that attempt to explore it are often ambiguous and epistemically problematic. That is, despite the huge amount of literature in insight-oriented psychotherapy and the many references found to the "self," "mind," "individual," "subject," "person," the meaning of the concept as an ontologically preexisting discoverable entity remains unclear. One may ask: "Just what is it that is being discovered in therapy?" Commenting on the meaning of the concept in psychoanalysis, Erwin indicates "[i]t would not be unfair . . . . to refer to the collection of psychoanalytic writings about the self as a conceptual mess" (1997, p. 41). Within the psychoanalytic literature alone, he identifies at least seven different uses of the term. The concept is used to refer to: "(1) a person, (2) the ego, (3) the mental apparatus, (4) a personality, (5) the core of one's personality, (6) a set of self representations, and (7) an inner agent" (p. 41). But despite the lack of conceptual clarity with the concept of self, insight-oriented psychotherapies assume it has an ontological status and claim the possibility of discovering its "true" nature, whatever that may mean.

Notwithstanding the conceptual mess surrounding the concept of self in insight-oriented psychotherapies, and the disregard afforded to the subtle differences between the terms used to characterize it—"subject," "individual," "I"—there remains a general and broad philosophical sense in which the concept is employed. As I have indicated insight for such therapies constitutes an unveiling of a "true," "core," or "real," self existing through time and which can be discovered. This idea suggests an understanding of the self or subject as an ontologically real entity distinguishable from the objects it experiences. As I detail much further in chapter four, it is an understanding of the self entailing an epistemological thesis characterized by "S knows that p" claims, where "S" is some subject discovering the object "p." As Friedrich Nietzsche would say, it is an understanding of the self that establishes a "doer" behind the "deed," separating the subject as that which experiences the world from the object (1887/1967, I, 13).

Such an understanding of the self, however, as some ontologically real entity discovering objects, stems from a certain world-view, characterized by a certain conception of knowledge and reality, that we need not accept uncritically. In chapters four and five, I consider in detail the epistemological and metaphysical aspects of this world-view, and show their questionable nature. In the present chapter, I will focus on the concept of self within this world-view, claiming its problematic nature undermines insight-oriented psychotherapy's reliance on it. In other words, if conceptualizing the self as some ontologically real entity discovering and experiencing the world should prove to be of concern, as I will claim it does, then insight-oriented psychotherapy's assumption of such a self is seriously undermined. If so, then is it not the assumption of such a self, rather than its rejection, that raises some serious ethical questions regarding the ideal of "mental health"? I will consider such ethical issues in chapter six.

Focusing on the subject as "doer," Nietzsche considered such an understanding of subjectivity as illusory, for "'the doer' is merely a fiction added to the deed" (1887/1967, I, 13).

> "Subject," "object," "attribute"—these distinctions are fabricated and are now imposed as a schematism upon all the apparent facts. The fundamental false observation is that I believe it is *I* who do something, suffer something, "have" something, "have" a quality. (1967, 549)

For Nietzsche, the supposition of some "subject" experiencing "objects" is illusory since it creates a false dichotomy in an otherwise singular field of experience. This illusion in turn posits a world-view wherein "subjects" and "objects" are considered ontologically real such that it is "I," as some ontologically existing subject, who does something, suffers something, has something. Such a representing subject constitutes a certain falsification for Nietzsche that owes part of its heritage to Immanuel Kant.

Although such an understanding of subjectivity originates with René Descartes, with Kant it achieves its clearest formulation, since Descartes still required a theological component, namely God, to complete his views on the representing subject. Only with Kant is God removed from the sphere of rational thought and considered entirely a matter of faith. Under Kant, the rational representing subject is divorced from any theological components in a manner and with consequences I consider shortly. For the moment, what is crucial to note is that with such a Kantian representing subject insight-oriented psychotherapy, and indeed contemporary thought, has the greatest affiliation. Kant articulated and developed an understanding of subjectivity in such a way that contemporary Western thought still revolves around the issues he indicated. The emergence of our contemporary Kantian understanding of subjectivity is thus recent. Although representation itself was not born with Kant, it is with him that it took a certain position in thought, which I consider below, with respect to its relation to the subject.

Before proceeding, however, it is important to note that I am not suggesting insight-oriented psychotherapy's conception of the self is specifically Kantian in all its details. Indeed, as I have indicated, it is not at all clear what specific understanding of the subject such therapies assume. What I am suggesting is that the idea of an ontologically existing subject experiencing and discovering the world stems from a certain history which, starting from Descartes and continuing through the early moderns, sees its fullest flowering in Kant's epistemology. And it is via this idea of the subject and not with the details of Kant's position that insight-oriented psychotherapy is affiliated with Kant. If, then, we undermine Kant's view of the subject and the consequent world-view it assumes, we also undermine insight-oriented psychotherapy's assumption of such a subject. That is, I am claiming the very idea of an ontologically real subject, which insight-oriented psychotherapy assumes, stems from Kant, who posits such a representing subject to satisfy the needs of his own philosophy. If Kant's position should prove to be questionable, as I will claim it does, then insight-oriented psychotherapy assumes and relies upon a historically problematic conception of subjectivity and its associated world-view. More importantly, with Kant, there were specific reasons, as I will detail below, that necessitated the postulation of an ontologically real subject, whereas with insight-oriented psychotherapy, such a subject is simply assumed!

A detour into the details of Kant's philosophy, rather than other early modern epistemologies that defend other versions of the subject/object dichotomy, is necessary to explain its suspect nature and to formulate a more precise understanding of why Nietzsche, quite correctly I believe, considered the ontologically real subject illusory. This is important because the alternative world-view I will propose throughout this study is Nietzschean in many respects and counter to Kant's position. Moreover, it is crucial to understand Kant's formulation of the "synthesis" required for knowledge, since in chapters four and five, the alternative Nietzschean "synthesis" I propose is in many respects a response to Kant and the world-view he articulated. However, although I have chosen Kant as the logical endpoint of a long tradition of thinking about the subject in a certain way, Martin Heidegger's (1927/1962, 1940–1946/1982) and Wittgenstein's (1958) critiques of Descartes's concept of subjectivity, in some respects do similar work to my critique.

Notwithstanding this need to consider Kant's epistemological views, the level of detail in which I will present them may be questioned, since I have claimed a lack of association between the details of Kant's position and insight-oriented psychotherapy's conception of the self. However, several important reasons necessitate a closer look at Kant's position. First, I want to avoid superficial and sweeping characterizations of the subject/object dichotomy which are often found in postmodern approaches. Second, it is crucial to show just how robust and deep is the subject/object split in Kant, and the sorts of problems it naturally led to. Third, and this is a critical point, the details of Kant's position show how complex and technically difficult is an apparently simple idea like the subject/object split—something which insight-oriented psychotherapeutic theories never explore.

In the *Critique of Pure Reason* (1787/1933), Kant begins by claiming that our experience of the world involves the formulation of various representations (A97). This formulation is evident in the Transcendental Deduction, in which he seeks to discover the necessary conditions for the possibility of experience, by way of representations. As he states at A97:

> [W]e must first of all consider, not in their empirical but in their transcendental constitution, the subjective sources which form the *a priori* foundation of the possibility of experience.
>
> If each representation were completely foreign to every other, standing apart in isolation, no such thing as knowledge would ever arise. For knowledge is [essentially] a whole in which representations stand compared and connected.

For Kant, the starting point is to inquire into those "subjective sources" which allow us to experience—that is, to formulate representations. Also, as is evident from the quotation, an experiencing subject is to constitute the point where this experience is realized: it stands as the entity that makes such an experience possible. As I will explain in much further detail below, such a subject is the entity which "receives" input from the world and processes it to generate representations. In itself then, Kant's starting point already assumes a distinction between the subject and the world. He begins with a world-view characterized by subjects who generate knowledge through representations, and whose a priori constitution he wishes to investigate. But why should we uncritically accept such a starting point? Why should knowledge, from the outset, be assumed as representational? These are important questions since they indicate a lack of any solid ground to justify Kant's starting point.

Starting from the assumption that we do have experience, Kant distinguishes between the passive and the active elements of our experience. Intuitions, the passive element, are blind without the categories and the various a priori features of the subject. Similarly, our a priori subjective abilities are useless without intuitions. "Thoughts without content are empty, intuitions without concepts are blind" (A51/B75). Intuitions constitute the raw material for the mind, and are of two kinds. Pure intuitions are a priori and are of space and time. They are a priori features of the subject, and are imposed upon all the empirical intuitions received by the subject. Empirical intuitions are "given" to the mind, and when processed, they yield objects of representation. Here "given" cannot mean "caused" since causality is one of the categories of relation. It suggests only that some input is somehow given to the mind. Also, by "objects of representation" Kant does not mean "objects capable of existing outside our power of representation" (A104). If we desire to discuss an object as existing independently of our mind, then we can refer to such an object only "as something in general = x" since we cannot know anything about such an object (A104).

We have yet to see how representations are generated according to Kant, but it is evident at this stage that he erects a strict dichotomy between the subject and the world such a subject experiences: a dichotomy with an historical tradition that insight-oriented psychotherapy simply assumes. For Kant, not even the notions of space and time are found in the world, but are imposed by the very nature of subjectivity on all that is experienced. However, for Kant, this assumed world-view does not seem problematic. As far as he is concerned, the task now is to explain the a priori features of subjectivity allowing for the generation of various representations.

Every empirical intuition contains a manifold which must undergo a threefold synthesis in order for a representation to arise. What Kant means by empirical intuitions containing a manifold is not quite clear, but the general idea seems to indicate that some input is given to the mind and must be processed in some way in order for us to be aware of representations. Beginning with what Kant calls a synthesis of apprehension, the manifold has to be apprehended in time where each single "time slice" will eventually appear as an element of an object. Thus, even though the represented object will appear as a unitary object, its different elements, as given in the manifold of the intuition, have to be apprehended in a time sequence because each "time slice" will contain a part of the manifold that will give the mind an "impression" of the object's various properties, and the mind cannot receive simultaneous impressions from any one intuition. Thus, as far as Kant is concerned, "in order that unity of intuition may arise out of this manifold . . . it [the manifold] must first be run through, and held together. This act I [Kant] name the synthesis of apprehension" (A99).

While the synthesis of apprehension is an extremely unclear notion in Kant, he appears to be suggesting the mind's inability to apprehend any given manifold without first apprehending its various parts. In other words, every empirical intuition contains a manifold which when processed provides a representation of an object. The manifold, therefore, "contains" in some sense the various properties of the object, such as its shape, size, and colour. According to Kant, the mind cannot simultaneously receive impressions from these various properties and must therefore apprehend them in a time sequence even though the represented object will be a single and unified object. As such, after apprehending in time the various parts of an object, these parts must be brought together and unified in order for a single and unified object to be represented.

Although the details of Kant's account may be questioned at this stage, it is important to see how complex an account Kant is developing in order to explicate the subject/object dichotomy—something which insight-oriented psychotherapeutic theories never provide. Although his place at the endpoint of early modern epistemology may assist in the provision of such a complex account, nevertheless, unlike insight-oriented psychotherapies, he does not simply assume a subject/object dichotomy without attempting to justify it in great detail.

For Kant, not only must a mind engage in a synthesis of apprehension, but it must also have the capacity for a synthesis of reproduction. In order for an object to be represented as unified at the end of this threefold synthesis, the apprehended manifold parts must be reproduced in an associative manner, according to some rule. The need for a reproduction of the different manifold parts of one intuition is quite evident. Since for any one intuition, its manifold is apprehended across time, the different parts of the manifold have to be brought together at one time if a single, unified object is to be represented at a single time. However, this reproduction is not accomplished through memory, or more precisely, through any memory that the subject is aware of (Brook, 1994, pp. 127–128). Since the subject at this stage has no representations, the reproduction of the various manifold parts must be an unconscious act of the mind, where the subject is unable to "recognise" anything in the process.

The final synthesis is that of recognition in a concept. The "manifold of the representation would never . . . form a whole, [if it were merely reproduced] since it would lack that unity which only consciousness can impart to it" (A103, my insertion). The apprehended and reproduced manifold must undergo a synthesis of recognition, which is an act that unites the manifold. Consciousness is here taken to mean awareness, or more precisely, a state of awareness, and is not an act (Brook, 1994, pp. 128–130). The synthesis of recognition is an awareness of the manifold; an awareness that imparts unity to the manifold and recognition in a concept. The fact that an object appears to us as unified is due to awareness imparting unity to the manifold of the object. It is of the nature of awareness to impart a unity to whatever the subject is aware of, and this is tantamount to recognition in a concept. This unification is what Kant calls the "unity of consciousness" at A105. It is "what combines the manifold . . . into one representation" (A103). The "unity of apperception" introduced at A105 is the unity of the act whereby a concept is applied to the unified manifold. Both the "unity of consciousness" and the "unity of apperception" are simultaneously applied to the manifold and thus, as stated above, imparting unity to the manifold is tantamount to recognition in a concept. Their difference lies in their relation to the manifold.

According to Kant, these three syntheses of apprehension, reproduction, and recognition, allow for the formation of representations. I have presented them in some detail to show clearly how their complexity and nature suggest that by the time we are aware of any representations, we are at quite a distance from the field of experience or the source providing us with the initial input. The gap between the subject and the field of experience is considerable, for three syntheses must manipulate any given manifold before we are aware of a single representation. Also, although the details of the syntheses are complex, they do indicate to us a part of the reasoning behind Kant's need to postulate an ontologically real subject, which at this stage has not been introduced. That there is such reasoning behind his postulation of an ontologically real subject is an important point to remember since, unlike insight-oriented psychotherapy, he offers a detailed account that culminates in a need for such a subject.

For Kant, the three syntheses do not alone provide the whole answer to how we represent objects since they only explain how we represent single objects. Our experience, however, involves the representation of many objects simultaneously. Thus, he now considers how it is possible for us to have such an experience, claiming that there must "be a transcendental ground of the unity of consciousness in the synthesis of the manifold of all our intuitions, and consequently also of the concepts of objects in general" (A106). Thus, the empirical synthesis and apperception require a transcendental condition. And "[t]his original and transcendental condition is no other than *transcendental apperception*" (A106–107). "This transcendental unity of apperception forms out of all possible appearances, which can stand alongside one another in one experience, a connection of all these representations according to laws" (A108). Since our experience does not normally involve individual objects but a whole group of objects simultaneously existing together, an act is required which allows us to have such an experience. This does not imply that we cannot concentrate on a single object at any one time, but that our awareness of this one object requires an awareness of other objects even though they may be in the background. For example, as I focus on the desk before me, I am also aware of a whole multitude of background objects such as the wall, light, carpet. The act which allows us to experience in such a way is transcendental apperception. It is transcendental because it is required for the possibility of experience. Thus, apperception has two aspects to it; an empirical aspect that involves individual objects, and a transcendental aspect that allows for the simultaneous experience of a whole group of objects. For example, apperception is required for me to represent the desk, and it is required for me to be aware of the situated context of the desk.

It is at this point that Kant believes he must postulate a transcendental subject, an "I," that is single and unified, and capable of ensuring that all experience belongs to this one "I." From A107 and A108, it is fairly evident that transcendental apperception is this "I." In these sections, Kant is quite clear about making a distinction between the empirical aspect of the self and the transcendental.

> Consciousness of self according to the determinations of our state in inner perception is merely empirical, and always changing. No fixed and abiding self can present itself in this flux of inner appearances. Such consciousness is usually named *inner sense*, or *empirical apperception*. What has *necessarily* to be represented as numerically identical cannot be thought as such through empirical data. To render such a transcendental presupposition valid, there must be a condition which precedes all experience, and which makes experience itself possible. (A107)

That Kant is here postulating a transcendental "I" is further shown by his reference to "the identity of the self" at A108. As far as he was concerned, for the possibility of experience, a transcendental subject is necessary. This is the "I" that unifies our experience and assigns it to a single subject. And since, according to Kant, no experience is possible without such unification, this "I" must be a condition for experience: it must be transcendental. What this subject is like, whether anything about it can be known, is another issue. But it is clear, at least from the Second Paralogism, that for Kant "we designate the subject of inherence only transcendentally, without noting in it any quality whatsoever—in fact, without knowing anything of it either by direct acquaintance or otherwise" (A355). Of course, we are still able to become aware of the subject empirically by introspecting our inner states, but this provides us with no knowledge regarding the "I" as subject of experience, for such an "I" is required for the very possibility of experience.

Under Kant's account then, an ontologically real "I" is required for the possibility of experience. Although nothing much about it can be known, since it is that which is required for knowledge in the first place, it must be ontologically real. Combined with his account of how representations are generated, a certain world-view emerges in which some ontologically real subject experiences the world through representations. That is, Kant's world-view consists of an ontologically real subject constructing representational knowledge through the application of certain syntheses. Leaving aside momentarily issues confronting such a world-view, and relegating to the background the construction aspect of knowledge, the world-view that emerges is that of some ontologically real subject experiencing the world and knowing it through representations. Although versions of such a world-view have been found in Descartes, John Locke, and David Hume, they receive their fullest exploration in Kant's philosophy. But from my earlier comments, such a world-view also characterizes insight-oriented psychotherapy's outlook. While I consider the details of insight-oriented psychotherapy's epistemological position only in chapter four, from what I indicated earlier it is fairly evident that this is its world-view. It is characterized by a subject/object dichotomy whereby some ontologically real subject is assumed as that which experiences the world. Note, however, that unlike Kant who offered a fairly extensive account leading up to the requirement of a transcendental subject, insight-oriented psychotherapies simply assume a simplified and unself-critical version of the subject/object dichotomy.

Kant's account, however, faces at least three issues which require consideration. First, there appears to remain for Kant a "miraculous harmon[y]" among the parts of the synthesis (Deleuze, 1983, p. 52). Although we are told how each part of the synthesis operates, no account is given of the harmony between each part. For some reason, Kant expects us to follow him in believing that there is such a harmony, without offering us any explanation for it. While he does not explicitly inform us of this expectation, it is implicit in his account. The three syntheses are meant to operate together in harmony to generate representations. Perhaps transcendental apperception is supposed to allow for such harmony. However, transcendental apperception is an act of unification. If it is to account for the harmony between the terms of the synthesis, then Kant must explain how such an act allows for the harmony.

Second, Kant does not offer us a "truly genetic" principle for the synthesis; a principle that requires no other principle to determine it (Deleuze, 1983, p. 51). Although, at A106, we are told that transcendental apperception is "original," we have no reason to follow Kant in accepting a transcendental condition as being itself unconditioned. For a truly genetic principle it must be a principle of internal determination in order to prevent a continuous demand for further justification. That is, it must be immanent within the field of experience without being logically situated as a precondition for the possibility of experience, since otherwise we can still inquire after a condition for the condition. In other words, unless the principle is immanent we may continuously ask for further justification.

Third, a more general objection can be brought against Kant regarding his distinction between the empirical and the transcendental aspects of subjectivity. As Michel Foucault notes, "a strange empirico–transcendental doublet" is created when man "is a being such that knowledge will be attained in him of what renders all knowledge possible" (1970, p. 318). For Kant, the transcendental aspect of subjectivity is what allows for the possibility of knowledge and yet, it is through our empirical awareness of subjectivity that this a priori condition is derived. Not only is the Kantian subject necessary for the possibility of knowledge, but it is itself an object of knowledge from which this a priori requirement is obtained. On the one hand, the subject is an empirical and finite object existing among other objects, and yet this same finite subject is the necessary condition for the possibility of all knowledge. If knowledge is possible only through the transcendental aspect of subjectivity, then how can we *know* this a priori condition through an *empirical* awareness of subjectivity? There appears to be some contradiction operating in the claim that through empirical knowledge we arrive at the a priori conditions for the possibility of all knowledge. How can we know what is required for us to know anything? It would seem that, at least, one piece of knowledge is possible without the a priori condition for knowledge—namely, knowledge of the a priori condition itself. If this is so, then not all knowledge requires a priori conditions: a conclusion which seriously undermines Kant's claims.

Kant's account, therefore, faces some serious problems. Although I believe he was right to insist upon the productive synthesis that produces knowledge, he was wrong to place the tools of production in an a priori synthesizing subject. Unlike Nietzsche, whose views I consider in the following section, Kant's inability to articulate a non-representational account of subjectivity and experience compels him to assume a synthesizing subject; an assumption which Nietzsche correctly considers "fictitious." Furthermore, his account ultimately subjugates being to knowing, further removing us from the field of experience. "What is" becomes "what is knowable," after the application of an a priori framework which allows for the possibility of representations.

If Kant's account is problematic, as I suggest it is, then what does this tell us about insight-oriented psychotherapy's assumption of an ontologically real self? As I have indicated, I am not claiming that insight-oriented psychotherapy accepts or is based upon a specifically Kantian position, but they do concur in postulating some ontologically real "I," together with the world-view it establishes: a view that Kant, more than any of the other early modern philosophers, most clearly articulated. In other words, I am tracing insight-oriented psychotherapy's conception of the self to Kant's transcendental "I" and the subject/object dichotomy it established. Although they would disagree on what can be known about such an "I," both affirm its ontological status. As Kant assumes a representing subject and inquires into the conditions that make such representation possible, so insight-oriented psychotherapy assumes some "real" or "core" self and seeks an unveiling of its life history. But, as indicated, understanding subjectivity in such a way raises several concerns. It is not a given "fact" that there is some "I" that experiences the world through representations, but an assumption articulated by Kant as that which makes all knowledge possible. In a similar vein, some ontologically real subject discovering the world through representational knowledge is simply accepted by insight-oriented psychotherapy as a given "fact." Consequently, insight and self-knowledge, as understood by insight-oriented therapies, rest upon an implausible understanding of subjectivity. It is not necessarily the case that some "true," "core," or "real" self is being discovered in therapy, but rather that such a self is assumed from the outset. The purported unveiling of such a self through therapy serves to reinforce the assumption, whereas in fact it *(re)constructs* the self it claims to discover. Perhaps, as Held comments, psychotherapy must assume such an ontological understanding of the self or individual if it is to function as a practice, but there is something unethical about passing along this assumption as the *discovery* of a "true" or "core" self since the process, in effect, deceives the client.

Not only does insight-oriented psychotherapy assume a questionable conception of subjectivity, it further assumes a problematic conception of self-knowledge as a backward looking process. To discover the "true," "authentic," or "core" self, the client must undertake a backward journey in time to discover those hidden causes and/or meanings that have affected an individual's behaviors, emotions, and personality. The "real" self to be discovered during therapy is allegedly constituted by its history which, when unveiled, is said to provide the client with self-knowledge and deeper understanding. Although history may play a less significant role under some modalities such as those that rely on existential philosophy, for example, it remains an integral part of the psychotherapeutic process for most clients, and serves as the gateway to greater insight and self-knowledge. In the example I presented previously, even under existential psychotherapy, the past was a tool, according to Yalom, in understanding the client's multiple sexual relations with other men.

Underlying this process of discovery is memory—especially painful memory—which serves as the key to past experiences, behaviors, and emotions, since more often than not painful memories are what trouble clients. Through remembering various experiences or events, and through an understanding of various causes and/or meanings associated with such experiences, a client supposedly gains greater insight and self-knowledge. Under classical Freudian psychoanalysis, for example, current emotional issues may be traced to repressed painful childhood experiences. Through re-associating what was previously an unconscious idea with its "proper" affect, the analysand gains greater self-knowledge and insight (Freud, 1915/1953–1974, pp. 166–204). Memory, as such, is crucial to the psychoanalytic process, as it is to other forms of insight-oriented psychotherapy. Ultimately, memory is what underlies self-knowledge in many such therapies. Note, however, that although there is a tremendous amount of literature on memory and its reliability as a source of knowledge particularly within psychotherapy, the point I wish to make does not question its reliability but its use in the first place.

It comes as no surprise to see that memory plays such a crucial role in insight-oriented therapies. For the majority of individuals, it seems as though there is no comprehensible way to articulate self-knowledge without some reliance, at least, on memory of past experiences and events. Indeed, as Ian Hacking remarks in *Rewriting the Soul*, "we have come to think of ourselves, our character, and our souls as very much formed by our past" (1995, p. 260). Our past seems to have become a basis for understanding ourselves and who we are. Without it, we become disoriented and at a loss, unable to function effectively.

But this reliance on memory as a constitutive element of self-knowledge raises some concerns, for memory is the breeding ground of negative, reactionary forces typified by such attitudes as resentment, guilt, and vengefulness. Indeed, such attitudes do not seem possible without memory. Of course, good memories exist also, but often it seems that negative memories play a much more significant psychological role for those who seek psychotherapeutic help, overwhelming any positive ones. Through recalling the past, and especially the painful past, these negative emotions are generated and regenerated, and are dragged along from day to day influencing and impeding all that a client may do. To borrow from Margaret Laurence's *The Stone Angel*, memories of the past are the chains we carry within us, and they spread out from us and shackle all we touch (1964, p. 292). But these are the very memories insight-oriented psychotherapy advocates as the route to insight and self-knowledge. I must remember, even if it is painful, for that is how I will know myself. And if the pain is too overwhelming, then I may seek the assistance of a therapist. But why accept an assumed, questionable conception of subjectivity that relies on the past as the pathway to self-knowledge? Why not consider the future as the pathway to self-knowledge?

Of course, I am not rejecting memory outright, for it may be necessary for knowledge, nor am I denying the benefits of good memories. What I am questioning is this reliance on it as a crucial component of self-knowledge, even if there were no dispute surrounding its reliability. Admittedly, many insight-oriented psychotherapies would perhaps identify memory as only one (perhaps central) component of insight; of little therapeutic value without a forward-looking and action-guiding understanding. Nevertheless, memory is still required to some extent at least before any forward-looking and action-guiding understanding is possible. But why not make the opposite force of forgetfulness a constitutive element of self-knowledge? Why not make forgetfulness a central component of insight and self-knowledge, and a means for a forward-looking and action-guiding understanding? As I will argue in the next section, self-knowledge need not depend upon memory, and may be articulated as forward looking, relying on the opposite force of forgetfulness. Again, however, I am not rejecting memory outright since forgetfulness still presupposes memory as that which is forgotten. What I am suggesting is a shift in the emphasis placed upon recollecting painful historical details as a means for greater self-knowledge. That is, I wish to discount the value of the painful past as a means to self-knowledge thus opening a space for a future oriented conception of self-knowledge.

Discounting the past in favor of the future is not a new idea. Indeed, what I am suggesting is similar to Nietzsche's account in the *Genealogy of Morals* where he advocates an "active forgetfulness" construed as a "positive faculty of repression" counter to memory (1887/1967, II, 1). For Nietzsche, active forgetting is necessary in order "to make room for new things" providing consciousness with "a little *tabula rasa.*" In fact, for him, "there could be no happiness, no cheerfulness, no hope, no pride, no *present*, without forgetfulness" (1887/1967, II, 1). Through active forgetting, which is ultimately an overcoming of the painful past; an overcoming of shame, resentment, guilt, and vengefulness, consciousness is allowed more cheerful future possibilities.

3. Reconceptualizing Subjectivity and Self-Knowledge

If, as I have indicated in the previous section, the Kantian inspired understanding of subjectivity is problematic for insight-oriented psychotherapies with their conceptualization of insight and self-knowledge which follows from their particular understanding of the subject, there remains the issue of how to conceptualize subjectivity differently and, consequently, insight and self-knowledge. Although I am critical of the subject/object dichotomy assumed in insight-oriented therapies, and their consequent understanding of insight and self-knowledge, I do not wish to suggest that insight and self-knowledge are not possible under a different way of thought. On the contrary, I do believe in the value of the ancient Delphic dictum to "Know Thyself." At issue though, is how to conceptualize the self to be known.

Under the Kantian inspired view as it is adopted by insight-oriented therapies, the self is defined through its life history and discoverable through an investigative process. But, as I have indicated, such a conception of the self ultimately renders being subordinate to knowing through representations. As was the case with Kant, "what is" becomes "what is knowable" by a representing subject. In psychotherapeutic practice, this subjugation of being to knowing renders what is considered as the "true" self to what can be known about it. However, any model that describes experience in terms of representations must of necessity postulate a realm distinct from the field of experience itself. In other words, representations of the field are not the field itself, which entails the need to postulate a realm for the representations. Thus, in a representationalist model of experience, a realm for representations must be posited. Representations are a re-presentation of something: thus a distinction is made between representations and what they are about. But as Nietzsche argued, all such models of representation entail a certain undesirable falsification of the field of experience itself; a falsification not stemming from an inability to accurately re-present experience, but from establishing a realm of experience—namely, the realm of representations—that does not necessarily change with any changes in the objects of such re-presentations. And given that the field of experience is a field in constant flux, which is Nietzsche's assumed starting point as it is mine, any representation of this field is bound to falsify it, for just as the representation is formed, the object has changed since it is a field in flux. Consequently, representationalist models of experience become suspect as a source of knowledge.

What is needed, therefore, is an account of subjectivity that does not rely on representations which subordinate the field of experience to what can be known about it. While such subordination does not equate knowledge with representation it nevertheless subsumes the field of experience under epistemic criteria. Along with Nietzsche, Foucault, and Gilles Deleuze, whose thought offers the least repressive account of the self—if we must have such an account at all—I wish to advocate the priority of this field, of becoming, over and above what can be known, conceptualized, or thought. My concern is for the very specificity of the empirical, asking for an account of subjectivity immanent within the field of experience itself. What precisely this means will become evident shortly. But my aim is to remain faithful to the field of experience in all of its richness. As such, we must not begin by seeking an account of how the sensible becomes intelligible, or by asking how a subject can experience the sensible. Our starting point cannot be based upon a distinction between a subject and the field of experience, asking how such experience is possible. We must begin with the field of experience itself, with becoming, asking for the possibility of a subject within such a field. Such an approach, however, is not phenomenological even though I share with phenomenology the value placed on experience. As will become evident, how this field of experience is conceptualized and what that entails, does not accord well with phenomenological thought.

Along with Nietzsche, who is the first to offer a systematic account of becoming, at least according to Deleuze's reading which I appropriate in this study, we may consider the field of experience as an ontological surface of forces where life, beings, matter, and all that we may call "reality" are already relations of forces; of "dynamic quanta, in a relation of tension to all other dynamic quanta" (Nietzsche, 1967, 635). As Deleuze comments: "Every relationship of forces constitutes a body—whether it is chemical, biological, social or political. Any two forces, being unequal, constitute a body as soon as they enter into a relationship" (1983, p. 40). Everything there is must already be a relation of forces which constitutes the field of experience as a surface in which types are located as particular constellations. Forces do not describe what is "real" behind the "apparent," but what is as it is. In chapter five, I offer a fuller account of this world-view characterizing it as "situated realism." For the present, I offer what I hope is a sufficient introduction to this world-view enabling me to situate a non-Kantian account of subjectivity within a non-Kantian account of experience.

Typically we understand the concept of force quantitatively. But, if forces have quantity only, then we are led to a mechanistic interpretation of forces which allows them to be equalised. That is, an equilibrium state may be achieved by equating some quantity of forces with another quantity. But, given the nature of becoming as a field of constant flux, there can be no such equilibrium. For Nietzsche, mechanism "desires nothing but quantities; but force is to be found in quality. Mechanistic theory can therefore only *describe* processes, not explain them" (1967, 660). Mechanistic theory, and indeed any description of forces that considers them only quantitatively, remains abstract and unable to explain differences in the union of forces. Under a purely quantitative description, there remains the possibility of equalising or annulling any union of forces. Thus, it is not possible to account for the forces in the union, but only the union itself, for there is no means to differentiate between the forces comprising the union. Hence, a purely quantitative description of forces can "only *describe* processes, not explain them." It cannot account for the different forces in the union. To explain processes, interpretation is required—an issue I consider in chapters four and five where this world-view and its corresponding epistemology are unfolded in greater detail. For the present, it suffices to indicate that the union of forces does not constitute a mere quantitative configuration, but one which is also infused with quality, with certain interpretations.

Given becoming as a field of experience, a field of forces in certain relations constituting diverse bodies—be they chemical, biological, social or political—how is subjectivity constituted within such a realm? For Nietzsche, we must understand subjectivity for what it really is: a union of forces forming a body. As he says in "Of the Despisers of the Body":

> But the awakened, the enlightened man says: I am body entirely, and nothing beside; and soul is only a word for something in the body.
> The body is a great intelligence, a multiplicity with one sense, a war and a peace, a herd and a herdsman.
> Your little intelligence, my brother, which you call "spirit," is also an instrument of your body, a little instrument and toy of your great intelligence.
> You say "I" and you are proud of this word. But greater than this—although you will not believe in it—is your body and its great intelligence, which does not say "I" but performs "I." (1883–1885/1969: 1)

This body, understood as a union of forces—a configuration forming a certain singularity—is situated within a matrix of other bodies, other singularities that are in constant flux. Rejecting any mind/body dualism, and any distinction between the "doer" and the "deed," Nietzsche's understanding of subjectivity is immanent within becoming as a singularity among many other singularities, constantly being configured and reconfigured. However, subjectivity for Nietzsche must also be understood as a "multiplicity," as an assemblage of different forces in relation to one another. As a particular body, subjectivity constitutes a certain singularity, but this singularity is itself an assemblage of forces dynamic within becoming, thus rendering any particular singularity also a multiplicity.

Critical to understanding the Nietzschean sense of subjectivity I am advocating is a rejection of the self as some "I" that traverses the field of experience representing it to itself. It is a rejection of any understanding of the self that posits some entity, some "I," with a discoverable history that allows for differentiating one particular "I" from another. Such an understanding necessarily subjugates the field to knowing, distancing us from the field of experience itself through the establishment of a realm of representations. Under the Nietzschean view, subjectivity is constituted immanently within becoming as a type which is itself fragmented and loosely comprised of a collection of forces. It is a certain configuration, at a certain moment, comprised of a whole multiplicity of differing forces. As a singularity, it is very different from the atomistic sense of individuation typically associated with that of a thing. As Deleuze and Félix Guattari comment:

> There is a mode of individuation very different from that of a person, subject, thing, or substance. We reserve the name *haecceity* for it. A season, a winter, a summer, an hour, a date have a perfect individuality lacking nothing, even though this individuality is different from that of a thing or a subject. (1987, p. 261)

But such an understanding of subjectivity, of individuation, appears counterintuitive to most suggesting the absence of any self. Surely, most individuals at least experience an intimate phenomenological sense of personal identity through which they recognize themselves. Similarly, most attribute such a sense to others and valuate other individuals on the basis of perceivable personal identity. With respect to insight and self-knowledge, intuitively, most understand insight about the self and the consequent knowledge gained as belonging to some "X," some self, that delineates a particular history unfolded through meanings or causes that may or may not fully capture this particular self, but are nevertheless defining characteristics of it. For example, if I am to ask myself "Who am I?" intuitively, I would expect the answer to reveal to me the meanings/causes associated with my previous and contemporary behaviors, thoughts, emotions, and personality. The assumption would be that there is some self, some Hakam, discoverable and understood through some previous history, as that to which such a history belongs. Although such an account may not capture me fully, it remains a defining component of who I am. And this intuitive understanding of insight and self-knowledge is what insight-oriented psychotherapy adopts as the discovery of a "true" or "core" self. They assume there is some Hakam to be discovered and understood. Moreover, in being counterintuitive to how most individuals experience their sense of self; does not this Nietzschean conceptualization of subjectivity remove us even further from the field of experience rather than being faithful to it?

While I do believe the Nietzschean inspired understanding of the self is counterintuitive to most, this is not because the intuitive phenomenological sense of self is a more faithful description of experience, but because most individuals are constructed and socialized from birth to experience through a subject/object dichotomy. In other words, our intuitive sense of self is itself a construction and not some pure description for there is no such description. This is why I am not a phenomenologist. Intuitively, most experience a certain sense of personal identity, characterized by a certain history, because their world-view necessarily imposes such a framework on experience. As such, the Nietzschean inspired view is counterintuitive to most since it situates subjectivity within an altogether different world-view not characterized by a subject/object dichotomy. In rupturing this dichotomy and maintaining a singular field of forces, subjectivity is not thereby abolished but rendered immanently within this field as a certain type of individuation. It is conceptualized as a certain configuration of forces, dynamic and continuously in flux with only a momentary identity established through relations with other bodies; other constellations of forces. In some respects, this view of the "self" relates to much older non-Western conceptions such as Buddhism, where the "I" as some fixed and permanent entity is viewed as an illusion human beings crave to actualize.

Under a Nietzschean sense of self there is no such entity as Hakam captured through some historical account. There is no unique set of traceable experiences unified under the label Hakam, nor is there some substratum that constantly changes. At any particular moment, I am but an intersection of various forces in relation to other forces that are continuously changing. Who I am with my family differs from moment to moment and from whom I am with friends, students, or acquaintances. What "individuates" me as any particular configuration at a particular point in time are power, perspective, interpretation, and valuation, all of which I consider in chapter five. But if this is the case, what sense of self-knowledge can possibly be attributed to such a self?

Unlike the backward looking understanding of self-knowledge found in insight-oriented therapies, with their reliance on memory as a tool for discovering the self, under the Nietzschean inspired self, self-knowledge must be understood as a forward looking notion relying on forgetfulness. Of course memory is required for forgetfulness since the past is what is forgotten. My point, however, is to shift the focus of self-knowledge from a lingering on the past to what future I desire irrespective of my past. This does not imply a denial of the past since it is through the past that I am at my present. Also, the implication here is not that anything is possible, for I am constrained by other forces which limit and restrict some possibilities. However, the *value* placed on what I have been and have done is far less than the value placed on what I can become. Here, the question "Who am I?" is not focused on the past, but the future, and on who I will become. To gain self-knowledge and to have insight into the self becomes an exploration of attainable possibilities—that is, future configurations of forces. Self-knowledge becomes the ability to know what one wants to achieve and how to achieve it, where "one" is understood as a configuration of forces. But since the future is always yet to come, self-knowledge here also means to know how to live deliberately, constantly creating one's future. However, since the self is but a loose configuration of forces immanent within becoming, living deliberately and creating one's future does not entail an infinite number of possibilities. It is the ability to re-evaluate and re-interpret a certain configuration of forces, aiming at the constitution of another configuration which must itself be re-evaluated. In contrast, those who lack self-knowledge live a life determined for them by their particular situation and the configuration of forces that constitutes them. Constrained by a focus on the past as a means to understanding who they are, the future becomes secondary to what their past will allow. Of course, some interplay between the past and future is possible, but the key point is how much value is placed on the past!

Although it is beyond the scope of this study to articulate fully the details of a future-oriented conception of insight and self-knowledge, it remains important to realize its possibility, albeit in a sketchy form. Perhaps with the notions of power, perspective, and interpretation that I unfold in chapter five, this account will become much clearer since it is there that I elaborate on force relations as power relations, and on how the quality of forces manifests itself as interpretation. My aim in this section, however, is simply to indicate that under a Nietzschean account of subjectivity, insight and self-knowledge are still possible. Since it is an altogether different world-view situating a Nietzschean understanding of subjectivity, self-knowledge and insight need to be considered from within this world-view. And within such a world-view they are possible as future-oriented notions seeking the actualization of various future possibilities rather than the so-called discovery of some past. Self-knowledge and insight become abilities to re-evaluate and re-interpret in order to constitute future configurations. Such a process does not entail establishing some future "I," reintroducing a quasi-Kantian understanding of subjectivity, but of ever changing and differing configurations that entail differing re-interpretations.

For most, this immanent conception of the self remains puzzling and is perhaps troubling due to the lack of any clearly identifiable sense of personal identity. Although I do identify it as a certain singularity, it nevertheless is situated within a flux that undermines any clearly graspable sense of identity. Thus, even the value I place on the future may be undermined, for as Mark Letteri has suggested to me through personal communication, I desire to be identifiable in the future in recognition of my strivings which not only requires personal identity, but also memory. Furthermore, at the interpersonal level, most would desire a clearly identifiable friend, lover, child, enemy, or acquaintance! The view of the self I advocate appears counter to any such relations and, more crucially, to the value I place on future possibilities. Surely then a stronger sense of personal identity is a necessary requirement.

As I have suggested, the Nietzschean inspired sense of subjectivity I am advocating indicates to me the least repressive account of the self. It radically undermines the fascism permeating the logic of identity which I explore in chapter four. However, this is not to suggest that a rejection of our "intuitive" sense of self and its associated subject/object world-view, necessarily leads to the position I am advocating. In *Human Experience*, for example, John Russon begins with a similar disavowal of our "intuitive" understanding of experience, advocating the primacy of interpretation "at every level of experience, from the most basic to the most developed forms of experience" (Russon, 2003, p. 11). For Russon, subject and object must be viewed as "a subject-object pair" defined through experience and are not prior to it. As he maintains, "[w]hat is first is a situation of experience in which all of the participants—subjects and objects—are already shaped and defined by the others" (p. 20). This situatedness of the subject-object pair, however, does not entail for Russon the position I am advocating, for although situated and mutually dependent, subject and object remain sufficiently identifiable for the construction of a personal identity.

Under the view I am suggesting, not only is interpretation primary, but the subject-object pair is itself ruptured and considered as a singular plane of forces where differing configurations of forces constitute bodies—be they chemical, biological, social or political. For Russon, such a world-view is "ultimately reductive" in its understanding "of the most definitive spheres of human experience" (2003, p. 3). Instead, he wishes to defend "the autonomy of the developed forms of human experience—of the 'self,' of 'truth,' and so on" (p. 3). Ultimately, it is a question of values, for what Russon considers as "the developed forms of human experience," I consider as the more repressive forms of human experience. Although Russon's analysis is more intimately connected with experience than the "intuitive" subject/object world-view, it remains distant from the field of experience through the categorization of a subject-object pair which delineates a certain personal identity.

Rejecting such a subject-object pair entails a much less repressive conception of self that is not articulated through personal identity but through personal *identities*. In other words, future possibilities become valuable for me not because I can identify myself in the future, but because of the multiple attainable identities which are not diachronically unified as me. In this way, multiple identities trump personal identity as the value I place in futurity. Thus, memory is not as crucial for the future as it may appear to be since it is not an enduring sense of self that I seek, but a proliferation of identities "freed" from personal identity. At the interpersonal level then, the sense I am advocating moves us away from human relations based upon identifiable categories—friend, lover, child—to relations between transient configurations and identities which, as I will discuss further in the next chapter, overcome the inherent "absorption" factor intrinsic to relations based upon a subject and object world-view. Admittedly, however, my conception of personal identities may appear troubling for most since not only it undermines much of our social and familial organization, but perhaps indicates for some a rather frightening and insecure future. Consequently, "personal identities" may be destructive rather than liberating!

In a certain sense, my conception of personal identities is indeed destructive in its attempt to undermine personal identity as an intuitively valuable dimension of human existence. For most, living a life of personal identities is a frightening rather than a liberating prospect since it is difficult to imagine a life based upon multiple identities. After all, personal identity as a defining characteristic of a being is ingrained from the moment of birth. Through various social and familial practices a newly born child is constructed as a being with a certain identity which is eventually internalized as a personal identity. To lose such an identity then, or to proliferate it into multiple identities, is a frightening and disturbing prospect. It is an unsettling prospect however, not because personal identity somehow captures some unique dimension of human existence, but because losing it or proliferating it entails a move towards becoming which amounts to a move away from being. Having lived a life at a considerable distance from the field of experience, from becoming, and having relentlessly attempted to establish a sense of being in the guise of personal identity within the flux of becoming, it is quite understandable why most would view personal identities as destructive. However, if my conception of personal identities is destructive, it is simultaneously liberating since it frees us from the falsification of becoming found at the heart of personal identity—a falsification that attempts to subsume becoming under being.

Ultimately, my critique of insight-oriented psychotherapy's understanding of insight and self-knowledge is a critique of the world-view such an understanding assumes. Characterized by Kant initially in its secular form, it is a world-view dominated by a subject/object dichotomy, where some "I" experiences and represents the world and itself. Such a world-view, however, stems from an inability to articulate a non-representational understanding of subjectivity and experience which necessitates, for both Kant and insight-oriented psychotherapy, positing some "true" or "real" ontological self. Although with Kant some philosophical reasoning is presented to account for the necessity of such a self, within insight-oriented psychotherapies an ontologically "real" self is simply assumed as a given "fact." This view is troubling, for this assumption is not typically questioned during the psychotherapeutic encounter, but serves as a foundation for insight-oriented psychotherapy's various practices. Consequently, as I will suggest in the next chapter, clients are "absorbed" into this view and its associated world-view, adopting it themselves as a given "fact."

Three

RECONSTRUCTION AND ABSORPTION

1. On Reconstruction

To an uncritical observer, insight-oriented psychotherapy appears as a tool of liberation and empowerment, alleviating suffering and seemingly increasing "insight" and "self-knowledge." And if such is the case, how can anyone object to so noble an end? But a close and critical analysis of insight-oriented psychotherapeutic practices reveals evidence to the contrary. Although suffering may indeed be alleviated, this does not appear to be due to greater "self-knowledge" or "insight," as they are understood by such therapies, but often to a reconfiguration of the client's psychological makeup whereby she or he unknowingly adopts the therapist's philosophical assumptions relating to the nature of the self, knowledge, and reality. From assuming a certain world-view at the very outset of therapy, a view characterized by the existence of some ontologically real subject experiencing and discovering the world, the psychotherapeutic process becomes one where such a view is reinforced and ultimately adopted by the client. In other words, insight-oriented psychotherapy's initial assumption of a discoverable "real," "true," or "core" self *becomes* real, so to speak, through the psychotherapeutic process. Such a "becoming," however, is a deceptive (re)construction, for clients are unknowingly led to believe in and accept newly "discovered" knowledge as knowledge of their "true" or "core" self. Moreover, in accepting and believing in the existence of some "true" ontological self, clients are also adopting the world-view associated with such a self which, as I indicate in chapters four and five, is a questionable world-view.

In the following section, I consider features intrinsic to and constitutive of the psychotherapeutic encounter, playing a significant role in reconstructing clients along philosophical lines similar to those of the therapist. That is, they are features which play a key role in reconstructing clients with epistemological and metaphysical assumptions similar to those assumed by the therapist. For the remainder of this section, I wish to examine the notion of "client conformity," since it serves as a valuable indicator of the (re)construction clients experience.

As I have suggested, contrary to the belief that insight-oriented psychotherapies apply a specific theory and method in order to discover the client's psychological makeup, such therapies assume from the outset both the existence of such a self and the possibility of discovering it. Through the psychotherapeutic process, they establish such a self by constructing it. One indicator of such construction is client conformity, whereby thoughts, desires, feelings, and behaviors are interpreted, molded, configured, and constructed to fit the particular theoretical and methodological assumptions of the therapist, even though they appear in the guise of "insight" and "self-knowledge" (Watters and Ofshe, 1999; Calestro, 1972; Rosenthal, 1955; McLeod and McLeod, 1993). Rather than counting as "insight" and "self-knowledge," as they are understood by insight-oriented psychotherapies, the features I consider in the next section, which include suggestion and power, together with the philosophical assumptions made at the outset of therapy, indicate otherwise. Instead of "discovering" themselves, clients "conform to the theoretical orientations of their psychotherapists" (Jopling, 2008, p. 153). This process is evidenced, as Jan Ehrenwald indicates, by the numerous occurrences whereby "patients undergoing therapy with Freudian analysts tend to produce Freudian dreams, Jungian patients to produce Jungian dreams, or Adlerian patients, Adlerian dreams" (1966, p. 108). In fact, Ehrenwald himself experienced this effect during his training in psychotherapy and psychoanalysis. As he writes: "During my Adlerian period my patients tended to produce characteristic Adlerian dreams. They gave way to more "Freudian" dreams during my subsequent prevailingly Freudian orientation" (p. 108). This experience indicates how clients have a tendency to grow into the specific therapeutic modality being applied.

While clients may believe they have "discovered" truths about their thoughts, feelings, and desires which in turn validate the therapist's theoretical and methodological approach, it is the therapy itself which has often "manufactur[ed] some of the very facts about the clients that [are] putatively uncover[ed]" (Jopling, 2008, p. 183). This process generates a "feedback loop" whereby insight-oriented psychotherapies become "self-confirming" (p. 183). They construct the psychological features they are meant to discover in the client, thus validating their own theories and practices (Farrell, 1981, pp. 126–128). It comes as no surprise then to find clients who have undergone therapy explaining themselves—their desires, feelings, behaviors—in terms employing the language of the particular modality applied to them, be it Freudian, Gestalt, or otherwise.

Typically, clients commence therapy with diffuse and unfocused desires, thoughts, and feelings, hoping that therapy will allow them to better understand themselves, and to bring a sense of order to an otherwise confused mind. The implication is that a certain degree of structure must be imposed upon such feelings and desires in order for them to be better articulated. And this structure is nothing more than the particular theoretical and methodological apparatus (including interpretations) the therapist applies. Of course not all clients are passive and accepting, but as the therapy progresses and the various constitutive factors such as suggestion and power, which I elaborate on in the next section, begin their work, the client's diffuse feelings and desires begin to mold themselves to align with the therapist's expectations, confirming explanations that the client would not otherwise have considered, such as a particular interpretation the client had not thought of. Depending upon how the therapist interprets, assesses, reinforces or dismisses a particular feeling, thought, or desire, the client is (re)constructed in a certain way. What were confused and diffuse thoughts, desires, and feelings, become focused and cognitively recognizable forces with associated intentional objects and unfoldable life histories.

Coupled with this initial philosophical world-view insight-oriented psychotherapies assume with respect to the nature of the self, knowledge, and reality, the psychotherapeutic process becomes one whereby clients are constructed or reconstructed since they enter therapy already constructed in a certain way. Fundamentally, such a (re)construction involves the client's adoption of and belief in the philosophical world-view assumed by the therapist. An indicator of such (re)construction is client conformity, with degrees that may, of course, vary from client to client. However, it is always present since at the very least the client must conform to the philosophical assumptions made at the very start of therapy. That is, even if certain specific interpretations made by the therapist are rejected by the client, at the end of a *successful* psychotherapeutic process, the client must at the very least be conforming to the therapist's philosophical assumptions concerning the nature of subjectivity, knowledge, and reality. Typically, however, it is highly unlikely that a successful therapeutic encounter would result in the client conforming *only* to the therapist's philosophical assumptions, for such assumptions are embedded in the therapist's questions and interpretations. And given the various operations of power and suggestion, it is likely the client would conform to more than just the therapist's philosophical assumptions.

Moreover, since a central aspect of therapy is the client's acquisition of a sense of agency, she or he is expected to take an active role in the therapy through self-changes. One form such changes may take is exhibited through a type of conformity whereby "clients explain their symptoms and therapeutic progress in terms . . . consistent with the theoretical orientation" of their therapist (Jopling, 2008, pp. 174–175). They manipulate their thoughts, desires, feelings, and behaviors so as to conform to the therapist's interpretations and expectations. In this way, not only does insight-oriented psychotherapy construct its subjects, but it also provides a mechanism whereby constructed subjects themselves reinforce the construction.

2. On Absorption

To better understand the constructive process at the heart of insight-oriented psychotherapy, we need to unveil those factors which are constitutive of the psychotherapeutic encounter as a dialogical encounter. Combined, these factors entail that the (re)construction occurring within insight-oriented psychotherapies is, in a certain sense, an "absorption" of the client into the therapist's philosophical framework. Since these factors are constitutive of insight-oriented psychotherapies, "absorption" is a term describing the change clients undergo in such therapies. Thus, "absorption" as that which results from the various constitutive factors within insight-oriented psychotherapies, such as suggestion and power, is itself constitutive of such therapies. However, before examining "absorption" any further, we need to consider factors constitutive of the psychotherapeutic encounter as a dialogical encounter, since their operation entails "absorption." Of course, although I characterize the encounter as dialogical, this does not entail it is a mutual, open, responsiveness between two people even though both therapist and client may believe it as such.

Intrinsic to the dynamics of insight-oriented psychotherapies are certain factors—mechanisms—that entail a process of "absorption." Although, for conceptual purposes, it is possible to demarcate these factors, in practice, they operate together as a single cluster of mechanisms, often in subtle and unnoticeable ways. They constitute primarily background forces of seduction through which a client adopts the therapist's framework. They do not, however, describe the philosophic nature of the framework being "absorbed"—precisely *what* is being "absorbed" and its problematic nature—which I will consider in later chapters. In this chapter, the focus is on some of those factors entailing "absorption." While I identify only four such factors, there may well be more.

A. Suggestion

It would be difficult for any insight-oriented psychotherapist to deny that suggestion, in some form or another, plays a role in therapy. Indeed, it may be said that the successful resolution of a psychotherapeutic encounter depends critically upon how well this factor—suggestion—has operated throughout. This criterion entails the claim that "the patient's suitability for psychotherapy is based on his potential openness to suggestions" making this mechanism crucial to the conduct of therapy (Strupp, 1972, p. 119). As such, this mechanism is not problematic, to some therapists at least, since it forms part of the psychotherapeutic process, even if it is not used as a deliberate means to convince or persuade a client to accept certain interpretations (Strupp, 1972; Schmideberg, 1939). If psychotherapy ultimately results in "veridical insight" the role of suggestion does not cause much concern. Commenting on its role in psychoanalysis, Sigmund Freud rejected its use as a means to persuade patients to accept interpretations they may otherwise reject. Such a misuse of suggestion would be conduct unbefitting to an analyst.

The danger of our leading a patient astray by suggestion, by persuading him to accept things which we ourselves believe but which he ought not to, has certainly been enormously exaggerated. An analyst would have had to behave very incorrectly before such a misfortune could overtake him; above all, he would have to blame himself with not allowing his patients to have their say. I can assert without boasting that such an abuse of "suggestion" has never occurred in my practice. (Freud, 1937/1953–1974, p. 262)

Of course we need not agree with Freud on this, especially given the rather superficial understanding of suggestion indicated in this passage. A much more intricate, complex, and subtle understanding of this mechanism is intrinsic to the intersubjective and dialogical nature of insight-oriented psychotherapies. A therapist need not deliberately and consciously manipulate and persuade a client for this mechanism to operate throughout the therapy. Body language, facial expressions, physical appearance, tone of voice, together with other factors I will discuss below, all contribute to suggestion and its powerful role in therapy. In fact, any intersubjective relationship characterized by some power differential would invariably involve some degree of suggestion operating in both directions to various degrees. This includes student/teacher, parent/child, doctor/patient relationships and many others. If by suggestion we understand a subtle cognitive, emotional, and behavioral influence on the client that is uncritically accepted or is perceived *as if* it were critically accepted, then Hans Strupp is quite correct in maintaining:

There is probably no therapeutic relationship in which suggestions, directions, and manipulations of rewards do not play a part. Stated otherwise, *I do not believe that a "pure" (nonmanipulative) psychotherapeutic relationship is ever possible.* (1972, p. 176)

But if "veridical insight" is questionable within insight-oriented psychotherapies, as I have indicated then subtle forms of suggestion do not constitute mere means to "veridical insight," but rather amount to mechanisms entailing the client's adoption of the therapist's standpoint. As such, suggestion's role in psychotherapy is of vital importance since it explains, in part at least, how a client is seduced (unintentionally perhaps) into conforming to the therapist's epistemic, metaphysical, and ethical standpoints. And this explanation applies to all the insight-oriented psychotherapies represented by the standard view, including the purportedly non-directive client-centered approaches. Indeed, in a study that focused on counselors who considered themselves client-centered in orientation, John and Julia McLeod found "a positive relationship between person-centered philosophy in counsellors (as expressed in their attitudes, beliefs and 'perceptual organization'), and their level of effectiveness with clients" (1993, p. 124). This finding indicates suggestion's role even in purportedly non-directive psychotherapeutic approaches, since otherwise there would not be a positive relationship between a counselor's personal philosophy and her or his level of effectiveness.

However, it would be incorrect to assume that subtle forms of suggestion are unidirectional in nature with no influence on the psychotherapist (Szasz, 1978, p. 98). The client's reported predicaments, response to questions, demeanor and bodily language all suggest to the therapist a certain way to react and a specific manner of proceeding with the therapy. But ultimately, it is usually the client who is seduced into the therapist's framework since it is the client who seeks change or relief from suffering rather than the therapist. Suggestion, as it is played out with the therapist, consists only in a means of providing the therapist certain cues on how to proceed with the therapy. As it is played out with the client, it masquerades as a means for change and relief from suffering. Moreover, the context in which this mechanism operates and the source from which it emanates is critical in determining the degree of influence and the predominant direction in which it operates (Calestro, 1972). With respect to context, we shall see below how the therapy is situated within a power differential where the therapist is perceived as the "healer" and the client is the suffering and vulnerable individual seeking help. This context, together with the perceived "high credibility," "expertise," "sincerity and trustworthiness" of the therapist (p. 87) indicate that it is the client who is more susceptible to suggestion.

Such susceptibility predisposes the client to various kinds of suggestibility, among which are psychological suggestibility and epistemic suggestibility (Jopling, 2002, pp. 134–136). Psychological suggestibility results from establishing close emotional ties with the therapist who is perceived as a higher authority figure. "This leaves clients more receptive to the therapeutic influence of the therapist in matters involving cognitive tasks and emotional responsiveness" (p. 134). Epistemic suggestibility operates on both the client's epistemic practices and objects of knowledge. "[C]lients adopt interpretive criteria and evidentiary standards that are the same (or similar) to those used by their therapists, which they would not have done had they not been exposed to therapy" (p. 135). Also, clients come to accept the therapist's interpretations of them, altering or discarding beliefs about themselves to conform to the therapist's interpretations (p. 135).

To these two kinds of suggestibility, at least two others may be added: metaphysical suggestibility and ethical suggestibility. By virtue of being epistemically suggestible, clients are also metaphysically suggestible, since accepting or conforming to certain epistemic standards and practices implicitly implies an acceptance of the metaphysical foundations that ground such practices. These include assumptions relating to the nature of reality and the self that ground epistemic standards and practices. In other words, clients adopt the philosophical framework or world-view assumed by their therapist. As such, clients in insight-oriented psychotherapies are subtly absorbed into believing in the "realist" metaphysics that grounds such therapies; an extremely suspect position as subsequent chapters will show. Moreover, the combination of psychological, epistemic, and metaphysical suggestibility induces an ethical suggestibility whereby clients tend to adopt values and ethical standards they might otherwise not have adopted. "Patients who improved tended to revise certain of their moral values in the direction of their therapists', while the moral values of patients who were unimproved tended to become less like their therapists'" (Rosenthal, 1955, p. 435). As Strupp correctly notes, "in successful therapy the patient tends to assimilate (identify with) the therapist's values" (1992, p. 399). I will return to this issue in chapter six where I discuss the ethics of insight-oriented psychotherapies.

B. Other Nonspecific Factors

While the role of suggestion in insight-oriented psychotherapies may be regarded as a nonspecific factor operating throughout therapy—that is, a factor not specific to any particular psychotherapeutic theory or methodology—I have considered it separately to emphasize its critical role. It constitutes, however, one nonspecific factor among many others found operating during therapy. I have stated in chapter one that at least four broad nonspecific factors operate in psychotherapeutic encounters (Frank, 1989, pp. 100–101). First, all therapies involve an emotional relationship with a therapist who is recognized as a knowledgeable and authoritative figure willing to listen and help. Second, all therapies involve a setting situating the client in an atmosphere considered both safe and indicative of the therapist's authoritative position as the healer. Third, they present some explanation for the client's symptoms and a procedure for alleviating them. And fourth, all therapies require both the therapist and client to participate in a process believed by both as beneficial. These factors describe how clients change and, together with the other mechanisms identified in this chapter, how they are ultimately "absorbed" into the therapist's framework.

The claim that nonspecific factors operate during therapy has been made by many therapists (Frank, 1989; Strupp, 1972; Calestro, 1972) and some philosophers (Jopling, 1998; Grünbaum, 1993). Borrowing from the various components they present, these nonspecific factors, together with Jerome Frank's four components, further include: the use of technically seductive language (Jopling, 1998); the therapist's respected position within the community and the pressures it generates for the client to accept her or his knowledge and authority (Calestro, 1972; Jopling, 1998; Wegrocki, 1934); the client's desire for consonance or for reduction of the cognitive dissonance generated by the therapeutic encounter (Festinger, 1957; Jopling,

1998); the influencing effects of the therapist's attitude, personality, charisma, conviction, and supportiveness (Jopling, 1998); the client's hope and desire for clarifications and interpretations to be truthful and accurate (Strupp, 1972); the powerful effects of rhetoric within therapy (Glaser, 1980; Frank, 1987); the client's adoption of the therapist's behavior as an example to follow (Jopling, 1998); the client's strong desire for symptom relief and the therapist's reassurance of its possibility; and the client's increase in hope and optimism when the situation may not warrant it (Jopling, 1998).

These factors combined and often operating in subtle and undetectable ways, contribute to seducing the client into the therapist's ethical, metaphysical, and epistemological framework. They are an intrinsic part of the psychotherapeutic encounter, continuing to operate in various forms even if their presence is made explicit to both client and therapist. For example, the influencing effects of the therapist's attitude, personality, charisma, conviction, and supportiveness may be made explicit to the client, with a cautionary note about their powerful role. However, this warning does not rule out their playing a part in therapy. The therapist will continue to have a certain attitude, personality, charisma, at play during therapy. With other nonspecific factors, such as the therapist's respected position within the community or recognized ability to "heal," it is unlikely the therapist's practice would continue were such factors eliminated. Indeed, as Barbara Held suggests, the ability to "heal" is a part of the definition of a psychotherapist (1995, p. 245).

Typically, however, the operation of nonspecific factors within psychotherapy goes unnoticed. Indeed, without the illusion of the standard view that change occurs through the application of a *specific* modality, it is likely that insight-oriented psychotherapy would cease as a practice (Jopling, 2008, pp. 85–86). Clients need to believe they are engaged in a legitimate and valid process of self-discovery and insight that can help them better to understand, cope with, and hopefully alleviate their predicaments (p. 86). Without this illusion, and with explicit awareness of the process as "absorption" into the therapist's philosophical framework and value system, insight-oriented psychotherapy would not likely be able to sustain itself.

C. The Role of the Question

As part of the overall mechanisms entailing "absorption," the role of questions in insight-oriented psychotherapies is central in explaining how clients are subtly seduced throughout therapy. Although both therapist and client pose questions, the client's questions, from the therapist's point of view, serve only to unveil the client's psychological and emotional state at that particular point in time, thus indicating to the therapist the various possible directions in which to proceed. The therapist's questions on the other hand, as the questions of the "healer" within the setting, *direct* the client in various ways that she or he might not otherwise have considered. The process, however, is more complex for an interplay of questioning between therapist and client directs the progression of therapy. This interplay may imply that the therapist's questioning has a limited role, for the client's questioning could, in principle at least, counter the directiveness intrinsic to the therapist's questions. However, given the role of suggestion, other nonspecific factors, and the power differential operating within the setting, the therapist's questions are most likely to direct the therapy.

For the therapist, a variety of different question formats may be used (Overholser, 1993). These include evaluative questions of the type "What do you look for in a marriage?" or "How would you rate your marriage?" (p. 68); memory questions such as "How often does the problem occur?" or "When it happens, how long does it last?" (p. 68); and others that may require interpretation, analysis, synthesis, or application. Whichever format the psychotherapist chooses, and no matter how careful she or he is in attempting to avoid directiveness, the very nature of questioning will direct the client along certain paths and not others.

By its very nature, questioning delineates a certain space from which an answer can be given. It posits a framework, a perspective which the listener must enter not only to understand the question, but to reply to it. Consider, for example, the question "How often does the problem occur?" It indicates not only that something is a problem, but that the frequency of its occurrence is significant also. In this way it delineates a perspective or framework whereby some "X" is a problem and its frequency is significant also. Of course, it is quite possible for the listener to debate the problematic status of "X" and whether its frequency is significant. But even in order to debate these issues, the listener must enter the framework posited by the question, for otherwise the debate cannot take place. However, for the listener these issues may not have been important prior to hearing the question. As such, the question has brought to the foreground a certain framework which the listener now needs to enter in some way. As Hans-Georg Gadamer states:

> The essence of the question is to have sense. Now sense involves a sense of direction. Hence the sense of the question is the only direction from which the answer can be given if it is to make sense. A question places what is questioned in a particular perspective. When a question arises, it breaks open the being of the object, as it were. Hence the logos that explicates this opened-up being is an answer. Its sense lies in the sense of the question. (1975/1989, p. 362)

If a question is to be understood, it must have a sense which conveys the point of view or direction or framework the listener must enter in order to reply. The framework indicated by the question demands from the listener an encounter with the question from within this framework if the answer is to make sense. As Gadamer correctly states, "[t]he openness of a question is not boundless" (p. 363). It is limited by the possibilities opened up by the question. To question is to establish presuppositions "in terms of which can be seen what still remains open" (p. 363).

Consequently, the very parameters established by the question constrain the "knowledge" that can be produced through the logic of questioning. The presuppositions of the question—be they epistemic, metaphysical, or ethical—establish the arena within which "knowledge" is produced. As Gadamer states, "[d]iscourse that is intended to reveal something requires that that thing be broken open by the question" (p. 363). It is the question that determines the parameters (constraints) of the reply not allowing for a response outside such parameters. Hence, the questioner—the wielder of power—determines the arena of "knowledge," perhaps posing at times pseudo-questions that merely reinforce her or his authority (Gadamer, 1975/1989, pp. 363–364).

Philosophers since Plato have known that the question wields tremendous power in determining the production of "knowledge," although Plato would not have referred to it as production. Indeed, Plato's Socrates made an art-form of questioning, employing questions as a means to lead the questioned into predetermined positions. He was well aware that questions determined the direction of the response. And it is to Friedrich Nietzsche's credit that he made explicit the axiological dimension of all questioning, for in indicating a certain perspective or direction and rejecting others, questions rank one perspective over another. For these reasons, it is not so much the question itself that is primary for Nietzsche, but *who* is asking the question: what values does the questioner hide within the question?

In insight-oriented psychotherapies, it is the therapist's questions—her or his epistemic, metaphysical, and ethical values—that determine the direction of the client's response. Through questioning, the therapist compels a client into a preconceived philosophical framework which, given the therapist's authoritative position, the client only too happily enters much of the time. And in entering, in responding to the therapist's questions, the client is in effect being drawn into the therapist's perspective—into her or his assumed philosophical framework. Although it may be true that many therapists, unlike Socrates, do not deliberately lead clients into preconceived positions, nevertheless, the nature of questioning itself subtly seduces the client often in the guise of offering her or him alternatives that she or he had had difficulties articulating.

But, borrowing from Gemma Corradi Fiumara's critique of Gadamer, what if the client were to respond outside the parameters determined by the question (2002, p. 135)? What if the client demanded a different perspective, rejecting the limitations imposed by the therapist's questions? First, the therapist would not be able to engage such a client, for the response would fall outside the sense of the question. Of course, the therapist may be able to shift points of view, but ultimately she or he cannot go beyond those philosophical assumptions that define the practice itself. For example, the therapist must assume some ontologically real subject if she or he is to remain an insight-oriented psychotherapist. Second, in a setting where the therapist represents the higher power, and where the client is suffering and in need of help, it is highly unlikely that such a client would be able to impose her or his framework onto the therapist since the perceived dysfunction of that framework is what brought the client to therapy in the first place. This inability, however, is not to suggest that every dimension of a client's cognitive framework is dysfunctional or unworthy of serious attention, but that even if the therapist gives it serious attention, it is unlikely to be adopted by the therapist in a *successful* psychotherapeutic encounter. Third, it is the client who seeks assistance in gaining "self-knowledge" and "insight" and is, as such, the object whose being is "opened-up" by the therapist's questions (Gadamer, 1975/1989, p. 362). Thus, it is highly unlikely that a client could even respond outside the parameters imposed by the therapist's questions since at the philosophical level such parameters define insight-oriented psychotherapies as a certain psychotherapeutic practice. Inevitably, in a "successful" psychotherapeutic encounter at least, the client is "absorbed" into the therapist's philosophical framework.

D. Power-Interpretation

As the standard view in chapter one suggests, "one of the primary agents of therapeutic change in the insight-oriented psychotherapies is the therapist's use of interpretations." Such interpretations constitute an essential part of the therapeutic process since they purportedly are the means through which a client gains "self-knowledge" and "insight." Without interpretations, no matter how minimal, it is difficult to see how the therapy could progress. While some insight-oriented psychotherapists may discount or reject the role of interpretations, interpretation is at the heart of any dialogical process. Whenever these psychotherapists speak during therapy, no matter how little, they are interpreting. In fact, as I outline in chapter five, interpretation is constitutive of "reality," and a manifestation of the quality of forces. The question of interpretation then, is a crucial part of the psychotherapeutic process, inviting a critical analysis of the various epistemic and metaphysical issues associated with it. This will be the task of chapters four and five. In this section, I wish to focus on the role of interpretations (and power) as mechanisms entailing "absorption"; as means through which the client is seduced into the therapist's perspective.

As such mechanisms, interpretations are perhaps the most seductive element of the psychotherapeutic process. If presented to the client at appropriate times in the therapy, employing an appropriate language, they become the hook onto which the client's suffering is hung. Their operation, however, cannot be understood adequately without an examination of the power relations at play throughout therapy. These relations, which manifest themselves through the therapist's interpretations, render this mechanism an intrinsic part of the psychotherapeutic process.

Power relations, however, are complex, and their analysis depends for the most part on the understanding or sense of "power" at play. One understanding of power utilizes a representative sense characterizing power as representing different positions of authority or strength. For example, in a student/teacher encounter a power differential between the student and teacher situates their encounter. In such a context, the sense of "power" utilized is representative in that the teacher *represents* a position of authority to the student. The student perceives this representation of power as does the teacher, and is constitutive of the student/teacher encounter. Such an understanding of power—power as representation—is clearly at work also in insight-oriented psychotherapies; an issue I will return to at a later stage. It is also the sense of power at play with the positing of questions, for the therapist's questions direct the therapy in virtue of her or his position as the healer.

But the therapist's interpretations in insight-oriented psychotherapy reveal another sense of power more clearly. Here, "power" is not so much representative power—as represented in the therapist's position—but *constitutive* power that emanates through the therapist's interpretations. In this sense, "power" is not a perceived representation through some office or position of authority, but it is what constitutes the therapist as therapist. It comprises the forces (or force relations) that form the complex "therapist" who is to conduct the therapy. As a therapist, an insight-oriented psychotherapist is an individual trained in a specific theory or combination of theories and in a methodology or various methodologies that attempt to apply the theory within a psychotherapeutic setting. With respect to representative power, the combination of this training and experience bestows upon the therapist a position that is perceived, by both therapist and client, as representing a certain degree of power. However, this combination of training and experience also constitutes the therapist as a therapist because the complex of power relations situates the therapist as a therapist within a particular community, society, and culture. They are the relations that individuate the therapist as a therapist and allow for interaction with her or him as a therapist. In this sense, power is constitutive of the therapist.

For philosophers, a constitutive understanding of power is nothing new. Nietzsche, Gilles Deleuze, and Michel Foucault are philosophers who have articulated power's constitutive role. But it is Nietzsche who first considered power as a constitutive element through his positing of a will-to-power. In chapter five where I consider metaphysical issues, I unfold a Nietzschean-Deleuzian understanding of power as a constitutive element of what I call "situated realism." For the present section, I wish only to indicate briefly how power is understood in its constitutive sense. In this regard, Foucault's Nietzschean remarks on power aid us in understanding its constitutive role, albeit not too precisely.

As it is constitutive of the psychotherapist, we need to understand power with Foucault "as the multiplicity of force relations immanent in the sphere in which they operate and which constitute their own organization" (1978, p. 92). Power, in this sense, "is the name one attributes to a complex strategical situation" (p. 93) which is the complex "psychotherapist" situated within a particular environment. However, although these power relations are constitutive of the psychotherapist, they

> are both intentional and nonsubjective. If in fact they are intelligible, this is not because they are the effect of another instance that "explains" them, but rather because they are imbued, through and through, with calculation: there is no power that is exercised without a series of aims and objectives. But this does not mean that it results from the choice or decision of an individual subject. (pp. 94–95)

What directs these power relations are the practices themselves in which and through which these power relations are constituted (Dreyfus and Rabinow, 1983, pp. 186–188). Within the psychotherapeutic setting, this practice—and not some conscious and deliberate effort by the therapist—compels the exhibition of forces constituting the therapist. That is, the configuration of forces constituting the therapist manifests itself. It is in this sense that power constitutes an intrinsic and critical aspect of the psychotherapeutic process.

As a practice with its own specific demands and rituals, the psychotherapeutic process necessitates the manifestation of those forces that are constitutive of the therapist. Such power relations manifest themselves through the therapist's interpretations which the client in turn adopts. In subtle and often unnoticeable ways, they manifest themselves as the therapist's epistemic, metaphysical, and ethical perspective into which the client is eventually drawn. From both the client's and the therapist's point of view, the resulting change in the client is due to "insight" and "self-knowledge." Both perceive the encounter as a situation wherein the therapist assisted the client in "discovering" herself or himself through a dialogical process. But, as I have indicated, such "insight" and "self-knowledge" are not "discovered" but constructed during the therapy. The resulting change perceived by the client amounts to an adoption of the therapist's philosophical framework. And, given that power constitutes the psychotherapist within the psychotherapeutic encounter, the client's resulting construction is a further manifestation of the power constituting the therapist. Consequently, although the client perceives the alleviation of suffering as a form of liberation, it is in fact "domination" by the power relations constituting the therapist.

As a psychotherapeutic practice, interpretation is a mechanism through which power dominates the client as it provides the illusion of liberation. Through interpretation, the client is gradually "absorbed" into the philosophical framework that constitutes the therapist. Without such power (understood as constitutive) the therapist cannot interpret for she or he would not be able to understand the client. By interpreting the client's experiences the therapist fosters change. But the therapist cannot interpret outside the very framework that constitutes her or him. As such, understanding the client's experiences and interpreting them amounts to a process of subjugation.

Combined, these four factors which I have just identified entail that the (re)construction occurring within insight-oriented psychotherapies is, in a certain sense, an "absorption" of the client into the therapist's philosophical framework. At the very least, the client emerges from a successful psychotherapeutic encounter believing in an ability to "discover" some "true" or "core" self, and in the world-view characterizing such a self. And since these factors are constitutive of insight-oriented psychotherapies, "absorption" may be characterized as a term describing the change clients undergo in such therapies. Thus, "absorption" as resulting from the various constitutive factors within insight-oriented psychotherapies, such as suggestion and power, is itself constitutive of such therapies.

There are at least two ways to describe "absorption" within insight-oriented psychotherapies. On the one hand, it can be considered as a conscious and deliberate effort to draw clients into a certain theoretical framework, a particular perspective that clients employ to unravel their thoughts, feelings, and behaviors. Here, the therapist is deliberately trying to assimilate clients by undermining their "autonomy" and prescribing the "correct," "true," or "healthy" way of thinking, feeling, and behaving. Fortunately, most self-respecting therapists reject this crude understanding of absorption, for it undermines the goal of client "autonomy." Although psychotherapists disagree on many issues, one that draws general consensus is the enhancement of client "autonomy" (Erwin, 1997, p. 1), which is typically understood as a certain sense of independence.

But another sense of absorption is much more delicate and more potent for client "autonomy," for it operates in subtle and unconscious ways. Here, absorption constitutes an unnoticeable process that draws in, engrosses, and engulfs without the explicit awareness of the parties involved. It operates by means of seduction through the mechanisms I identified, with neither the seducer nor the seduced being aware of the activity. In this sense, absorption engenders an unintended engulfment that is more potent than its crude variety because of its hardly detectable operation. And this sense of absorption plagues insight-oriented psychotherapies despite their endorsement of client "autonomy."

Through the operation of the mechanisms I identified, which are *intrinsic* to the practice of insight-oriented psychotherapies, subtle and unintentional absorption seduces the client into a philosophical framework that subsequently situates her or his thoughts, feelings, and behaviors. The client views this absorption as "self-knowledge" and "insight," for she or he is mostly unaware of the subtle mechanisms operating throughout the therapy. Similarly, for the therapist, it *seems* as though therapeutic change results from the client's "discovery" of some "true" aspects relating to her or his "core" self, when in fact such a self is assumed at the outset, thus rendering such a "discovery" a construction. This view of the client, however, is not meant to suggest that most therapy clients are easily gulled into a passive compliance. On the contrary, many clients are skeptical, questioning, intelligent, deliberative individuals. But despite such qualities, the extremely subtle and elusive nature of the mechanisms I identified inevitably leads to the absorption of clients in a *successful* therapeutic encounter.

What facilitates this subtle absorption are certain positions occupied by both client and therapist at the commencement of therapy. Focusing on the client, she or he usually decides to seek the help of a psychotherapist to alleviate suffering of some form or another. Not surprisingly, such a client who has reached a state of disillusionment and seeks a solution is perhaps willing to accept any change that would reduce the suffering. The client, therefore, may enter the therapy in a very vulnerable position, with a sense of powerlessness, having arrived there only after deciding that self-help was impossible. Greeting such a client is a psychotherapist whom the client considers a knowledgeable professional, able and willing to help. More importantly, however, the therapist's position as an authoritative healer confers upon her or him an overwhelming degree of representative power that the client only too happily accepts, since it creates a faith in therapeutic capacities to alleviate the suffering.

Therefore, a power—that is, representative power—differential exists at the very outset of therapy and pervades succeeding sessions. Without such a differential, it seems highly unlikely that the therapeutic encounter would take place. A client must perceive a therapist as possessing a greater degree of power and ability than she or he (the client) can claim in order to seek the help. Moreover, a client must be willing to accept this position of power—as a specific theory and method—in order for the therapy to commence. Given the client's vulnerable state and the therapist's authoritative position, such a power differential invites and facilitates absorption in insight-oriented psychotherapies. It creates space for the four mechanisms identified previously to operate in the guise of "insight" and "self-knowledge."

Of course, the general view that a vulnerable, suffering, and disillusioned person is more easily attracted into a framework or world-view that promises "truth" and "insight," and reduces suffering, is not restricted to insight-oriented psychotherapies nor to psychotherapy as a whole. For example, Kathryn Fox examines a Cognitive Self-Change program in prison demonstrating "the ways in which the institutional discourse of CSC coercively constructs new selves for inmates and the inmates' responses to these constructions" (2001, p. 176). Also, Donileen Loseke examines support groups for "battered women" where their identities are transformed along "familiar institutional identities" (2001, p. 108). On another front, many religious, political, and social organizations have relied on individuals' vulnerability and disillusionment as key to successful recruitment, although in most such cases the absorption is intentional and deliberate.

At an even broader level, the process of subjugation intrinsic to psychotherapeutic practice is evident in all human relations characterized and situated within a subject/object dichotomy. As long as such relations are construed as relations between subjects with a personal identity, power inevitably leads to a clash among such subjects, each desiring to absorb and dominate the other. And this process is evident even if we conceptualize subject and object as "a subject-object pair" defined through experience (Russon, 2003). Recognizing the inevitable power struggles in human relations, John Russon suggests "[a] successful resolution to the tensions of intersubjective life" through "the project of cooperation" which entails "collections of people adopting similar views about the order of things and consequently behaving toward each other out of a shared sense of what constitutes the reality of their world" (p. 60). But what this "successful resolution" amounts to, as is evident throughout Russon's discussion of the family and social life, is an absorption into a community of shared values which is the manifestation of a process of subjugation. To overcome such a process then, we need to move away from personal identity towards personal identities, as I suggest in the previous chapter. Through such a move, we do not eliminate subjugation since power is constitutive, but lessen its impact in human relations, for such relations are no longer viewed as struggles between subjects with a certain personal identity. Under the vision I am proposing, "human" relations become relations between *identities* which are always partial, incomplete, fragmented, and in flux.

While insight-oriented psychotherapists, I believe, are motivated by virtuous ends desiring to alleviate suffering and improve clients' lives, their assumed world-view coupled with factors intrinsic to the psychotherapeutic encounter result in the (re)construction of clients, rather than the client's "discovery" of "truths" about the self. But we have yet to see in detail why insight-oriented psychotherapists' assumed world-view is suspect, and how the very notion of "knowledge as discovery" is itself problematic. So far, I have focused on the psychotherapeutic encounter itself, suggesting that the assumption of a "real" or "core" self at the outset of therapy, coupled with factors intrinsic to and constitutive of the psychotherapeutic encounter, entail the (re)construction of clients during therapy. Now, I would like to focus on the philosophical framework psychotherapists assume in order to show its dubious nature. More specifically, I would like to shift our attention to the conception of knowledge assumed by insight-oriented psychotherapists and the consequent metaphysical view associated with such a conception. If it turns out that the very idea of "knowledge as discovery" is questionable, as I will claim it is, then this adds further support to the claims of this chapter.

Four

EPISTEMOLOGICAL ISSUES

1. Knowledge as Discovery

My analysis in the previous chapters suggests that, contrary to their self-presentation insight-oriented psychotherapies are not engaged in a process whereby some "true" or "core" self is discovered, but in a dialogical exchange that assumes the existence of some "core" self at the outset. This assumption, coupled with factors constitutive of psychotherapeutic practice, such as suggestion and power, entails that the client is constructed through the therapeutic process in such a way that she or he is absorbed into the psychotherapist's philosophical framework. The nature of this framework and the problematic philosophical assumptions underlying it will be the focus of the present and the following chapter. Before engaging this discussion, however, it is crucial to note that even *if* the philosophical framework clients are absorbed into is not problematic, insight-oriented psychotherapies are still involved in a form of deception. By claiming to provide a means of discovering some "true" self when in fact they are constructing one, such therapies are deceiving clients into believing in a "true" or "core" self when such a self is only an assumption: an assumption of the very practices that claim to find it. This charge in itself, to which I will return in chapter six, seriously undermines insight-oriented psychotherapies. For the present, I wish only to emphasize that the questionable nature of the philosophical framework clients are absorbed into, in both its epistemological and metaphysical aspects, serves further to undermine what is already a deceptive set of practices.

In chapter three, I claimed insight-oriented psychotherapies are engaged in a process which entails the absorption of clients into the therapist's philosophical framework. By this, I do not mean clients somehow become copies of the therapist they are engaged with, adopting her or his particular attitudes, beliefs, and values, but that they are, at the very least, drawn into the philosophical framework or world-view situating such attitudes, beliefs, and values. And fundamentally, such a framework or world-view is characterized by certain presuppositions about the nature of knowledge and reality. However, this claim does not imply that none of the therapist's attitudes, beliefs, and values are adopted by the client. Indeed, in chapter three I suggested otherwise. Perhaps it is best to consider the degree of client absorption, in a *successful* psychotherapeutic encounter, as a continuum where one extreme renders the client a copy of the therapist, and the other amounts to an adoption of the therapist's presuppositions about the nature of knowledge and reality. In most cases, it is likely that clients would be partially influenced by the therapist, thus occupying a position somewhere along such a continuum. Minimally, they adopt the therapist's epistemological-metaphysical presuppositions. Put differently, insight-oriented psychotherapists, whether implicitly or explicitly, assume a certain epistemological and metaphysical stance that situates their practices and is transferred to the client during the course of therapy. Their particular understanding of the nature of knowledge and reality, which is assumed as "correct" or "true," is *implicitly* adopted by the client as the "correct," "true," or "healthy," worldview. In this way the client is absorbed into the therapist's philosophical framework. But as this chapter and the next will demonstrate, this framework is itself highly suspect.

Focusing first on the epistemological dimension in this chapter, it is exceedingly difficult to find a clear articulation of the epistemological assumptions of insight-oriented psychotherapists. This difficulty is understandable however because they are not philosophers, and are therefore not expected to provide clear formulations of their epistemological and metaphysical positions. But from the standard view presented in chapter one and the assumptions such therapies make about the nature of subjectivity, as presented in chapter two, their epistemological assumptions become fairly evident.

Recall part (1) of the standard view I outline in chapter one: "Insight-oriented psychotherapy is a valid method of personal discovery that allows clients to discover truths about themselves, and to acquire bona fide self-knowledge." This, according to David Jopling, constitutes the principle of exploratory validity common to all insight-oriented psychotherapies (2008, p. 72). Unfolding this principle, Jopling comments that insight-oriented psychotherapy

> affords clients the opportunity for discovering certain salient facts about themselves: viz. facts about their personality, behaviors, emotions, interpersonal relations, motives, and developmental history, as well as facts about the etiology of their target disorders. These facts exist prior to therapeutic exploration in the same way that the facts of geography exist prior to exploration. (p. 72)

These facts, as Jopling indicates, are "logically independent of the specific theoretical framework" which is only a means to identify and describe them (p. 72). Consequently, the facts discovered "are logically independent of the treatment methods and exploratory procedures brought to bear upon them" (p. 72). Accordingly, insight-oriented psychotherapies maintain an epistemological position that clearly demarcates a realm where facts are awaiting discovery. The task of the psychotherapeutic process is to assist in the discovery of such facts, thus allowing the client to attain greater self-knowledge.

As such, insight-oriented psychotherapy is a means of discovering facts that exist independent of or are prior to any particular theoretical orientation. The objects of the knowledge such therapies seek are "out there" awaiting discovery.

Coupled with its assumptions about the nature of subjectivity—that there is some "core" or "true" self awaiting discovery—insight-oriented psychotherapy's epistemological assumptions become fairly evident: self-knowledge constitutes a process whereby the "right" theoretical and methodological tools are applied in order to discover certain preexisting facts about the self. These facts are *not* constructed through therapy, but *discovered*. In classical psychoanalysis, for example, the appeal to discovered facts is evident in Sigmund Freud's archaeological metaphor: the psychoanalyst resembles the archaeologist who excavates past histories (1937/1953–1974, p. 259). Similarly in existential therapy, the facts discovered include the client's choices, moods, projects, and attitude towards death. Also, in existential philosophy, as with Jean-Paul Sartre for example, we find frequent reference to "facticity," which suggests a certain factuality about the individual that cannot be wished away or avoided in an act of choice. Although no such factuality fully determines an individual, it is an integral part of her or him that can not be denied. Consider Sartre's account of the homosexual in bad faith (1943/1956, pp. 107–112). For Sartre, this is a man who would not consider himself "a paederast" even though he has engaged in such acts. What Sartre means by "bad faith" need not concern us here, but the suggestion is that the man's acts are certain facts about him.

Consequently, existential psychotherapy is not immune to my critique of insight-oriented psychotherapy. While it is true, as I have suggested previously, that history may play a less significant role under this specific modality, this does not imply that existential psychotherapy is oblivious to past experiences nor that it does not seek to discover certain facts throughout the therapy. Moreover, even though the client is considered in terms of being-in-the-world, as Ernesto Spinelli suggests, there remains a dichotomy between self and world whose inter-relations are explored throughout the therapy (Spinelli, 2005, pp. 144–145). Exploring the fundamental aims and objectives of existential psychotherapy, Spinelli maintains that

> if there is an ultimate aim to existential psychotherapy, it is to offer the means for persons to examine, confront, clarify and reassess their understanding of life, the problems encountered throughout their life, and the limits imposed upon the possibilities inherent in being-in-the-world. (p. 145)

Such an examination is a "revealing investigation of one's inter-relationally derived worldview" (p. 145) where the focus is on "descriptive components rather than . . . theory-driven interpretations" (p. 146). Ultimately, such descriptive components *reveal* "the client's self/world relations" (p. 146) which may then be "examined, challenged and reconsidered in relation to the problems encountered throughout their lives" (pp. 145–146). Clearly then, for Spinelli at least, not only is there a distinction between self and world, but despite the focus on present relations the past still has a role in therapy which is indicated through Spinelli's frequent references to "throughout their lives." Moreover, through his distinction between description and interpretation and how the former is revealed throughout the therapy, he indicates a process of discovery at the very heart of existential psychotherapy.

A possible objection to my characterization of insight-oriented psychotherapy's epistemological position may suggest that the object of knowledge discovered in such therapies differs from objects such as tables and chairs. Consequently, I should not draw a parallel between the two kinds of knowledge. In reply, I suggest that although in insight-oriented psychotherapy the emphasis is on self-knowledge rather than on knowledge of objects in general—such as tables and chairs—it is difficult to see how its epistemological position with respect to objects in general would differ. In other words, if the object of self-knowledge is something that is discovered as a fact rather than constructed, it would be difficult, if not inconsistent, to claim a construction rather than a discovery of objects in general. What would such an account be like? Furthermore, given the dialogical process required for self-knowledge within the psychotherapeutic setting in which another individual is required as a participant in discovering the client's "true" self, the object of knowledge here does not appear that different from knowing such items as tables and chairs. In both cases the object of knowledge is a fact "out there" awaiting discovery. Consequently, insight-oriented psychotherapy's epistemological position regarding the nature of self-knowledge stems from the broader epistemological claim that knowledge is a matter of discovery. And this is the epistemological framework situating insight-oriented psychotherapies.

That insight-oriented psychotherapies do assume such an epistemological position, of course, comes as no surprise since in chapter two, where the focus was on the subject of such knowledge, I suggested insight-oriented psychotherapy's conception of the self or subject is as an ontologically real entity distinguishable from the objects it experiences, and it functions as that which represents objects. With such a dichotomy between the subject and the objects it represents, it is not surprising that insight-oriented psychotherapy's epistemological position would include such objects as facts awaiting discovery. Moreover, insight-oriented psychotherapy is not alone in maintaining such an epistemological position. Indeed, the thesis that objects are discoverable is perhaps the mainstream position within and outside the academy, and is that of empirical science and many other disciplines. But what exactly is the nature of this widely accepted epistemological position?

The idea is quite simple: the discovery of facts about the world constitutes knowledge! To know "p" is the case is to have some "S" discover this fact in such a way that any subject may be this "S." As a discoverable fact, "p" is independent of "S" and uncontaminated by it, if "p" is known objectively. For mainstream epistemology, this view defines knowledge as justified true belief. For example, for me to know "z," "z" must actually be the case; I must believe that it is the case; and I must be justified in my belief in "z." Often, criteria are sought for justification, asking for what would justify my belief in "z." Two critical components constitute this epistemological view. First, the subject of such knowledge, the "S," has no influence or impact on what is known except in so far as it is the subject that knows. If there is influence by the subject, then it can be factored out. The particular circumstances or situation of the subject have no relation to what is known, for if "p" is to be *known*, any subject may know it. Second, objectivity under this view implies that nothing unique to the knower influences what is known. If, for example, the knower's emotional state plays a role in what is discovered, then objectivity is compromised or even destroyed. However, this is not to imply that knowers are infallible, for mistakes may occur, but that objectivity demands a denial of the knower's particular situatedness, including her or his emotions.

Within insight-oriented psychotherapy, both of these components play a significant role. First, the therapeutically relevant facts discovered are independent of the particular theoretical and methodological apparatus applied. Furthermore, these facts are independent of the particular attitudes or beliefs of both client and therapist. A fact about a client remains a fact regardless of whether the client and/or therapist know it. Second, an important goal of therapy is objectively to discover facts pertaining to the "real" self. And in order for the knowledge to be objective and uncontaminated, the personal biases of both client and therapist must be put aside or worked through for the facts to be discovered.

Consider, for example, Freud's remarks on the workings of repression. In a 1915 paper, Freud clearly positions himself against the notion of unconscious affects: "Strictly speaking . . . there are no unconscious affects as there are unconscious ideas" (1915/1953–1974, p. 178). As far as he was concerned, a distinction should be made between the affect and its associated idea. What may become unconscious, through repression, is the idea associated with the affect, and it is because of the affect that the idea is repressed. The first step in repression involves isolating the idea from its affect. The idea becomes unconscious, while the affect, "[o]wing to the repression of its proper representative [is] forced to become connected with another idea, and is now regarded by consciousness as the manifestation of that idea" (pp. 177–178). Alternatively, the affect may remain as it is in consciousness, whether wholly or in part; or it may be "transformed into a qualitatively different quota of affect, above all into anxiety" (p. 178); or it may be suppressed and prevented from developing.

Regardless of what occurs to the affect after it is split from its corresponding idea, the task of psychoanalysis is to re-associate the affect with its proper idea in order, for example, to overcome anxiety. And this is a process of discovering which affect corresponds with which idea. That affect "k" corresponds to idea "w" in client "S" is a fact independent of both what the analysand believes and who is conducting the analysis. Also, in order to discover this piece of knowledge, other affects must be worked through during the analysis so as not to contaminate the discovery. Both analyst and analysand need to ascertain that affect "k" and not "u" corresponds to idea "w." And as indicated in chapter one, through therapeutic improvement, insight-oriented psychotherapies ascertain the discovery of a fact as true of the self in question. If no therapeutic improvement is observed, then either no fact has been discovered or what has been unveiled is contaminated by other factors.

From the client's perspective, the alleviation of symptoms indicates a positive therapeutic outcome. As far as she or he is concerned the process has worked and the symptoms are virtually gone! For the psychotherapist of course this improvement validates the particular theoretical and methodological tools applied, and all seems well. The client emerges from therapy having gained greater insight and self-knowledge through discovering herself or himself. And the client must believe in these facts and in this discovery if the psychotherapeutic process has been successful. Indeed, a necessary component of therapeutic improvement is the client's belief and acceptance of the discovered facts. But to accept such facts—to accept that they have been discovered, thus not manufactured or instilled—is to accept also the epistemological assumptions that underlie any claim to the discovery of facts. In other words, accepting and believing in the discovery of facts assumes acceptance of an epistemology that construes knowledge as the discovery of facts. The client, in accepting the results of the psychotherapeutic process and believing in the newly found "knowledge," implicitly accepts the epistemological framework situating such knowledge. In other words, the client must necessarily be accepting an epistemological framework that considers knowledge as discovery. Of course, whether the client knows she or he is accepting such an epistemological framework, is another question, and is an empirical one. For the client, this is not only the road to greater insight and self-knowledge but, more importantly, it is the road to "health," since the symptoms have been alleviated. And what can be a greater motivator for someone to believe than the successful removal of their pain and suffering?

2. Critique

Perhaps if the epistemological framework clients are absorbed into were not problematic, my concerns would diminish. But such is not the case. Indeed, from my critique in chapter two, which focused on the subject supposedly discovering such knowledge, it is evident that insight-oriented psychotherapy's epistemological assumptions are questionable. Since such therapies rely on knowledge claims of the form "S knows that p," if their conception of "S" is suspect, it is likely that their conception of "p" as the object is suspect also. Having focused on the nature of subjectivity in chapter two, I turn my attention to the "object" in this chapter.

As I have indicated, a fundamental component of insight-oriented psychotherapy's epistemological stance is that subjective factors particular to the knower are irrelevant to the discovery of objects. The objects of knowledge are considered as facts to be known objectively, without contamination by the knower. Subjective factors such as emotions, feeling, values, need to be relegated to the side so as not to infringe upon the discovery of facts. Implicit within such an epistemological outlook is the belief in a required "permanence" or partial "permanence" at least with respect to objects of knowledge. That is, objects of knowledge must have some determinate and (re-)identifiable properties. But by permanence I do not mean a hurricane or an extinct species cannot be known. My suggestion is that in order for someone to *know* an object, it must be fixed in some way and delineated as an independent thing to be known (discovered). Both subject A and B may know c since discovering c is independent of A and B, and it remains c for some finite length of time. It is fixed or permanent in some definite sense. Subjective factors unique to A or B would introduce an element of change or flux if they were to constitute a part of knowing c.

Historically, the idea that knowledge or truth pertains to what is fixed and unchanging rather than to what is in flux and changing, may be traced back to the Presocratics, but it is Plato who has had the greatest historical influence with this idea. For him, truth and knowledge were not found in the realm of experience since within this realm of space and time all was in flux and constantly changing. This realm of appearances, of becoming, could not yield knowledge, which required permanence and fixity. Thus, Plato sought knowledge in a realm beyond space and time, in being, where reality remains fixed and permanent. This is the realm of Plato's Forms. But within the realm of appearances, of copies, Plato made another distinction between appearances with a close relation to being and those very distant from being. He distinguished within becoming as a whole those copies with a relation to the Forms and those distantly related that were copies of the copies (*Republic*, 509e–510a). As copies of copies, items at this level constituted a realm of shadowy likenesses that for Plato were distant from the Forms' action

(*Philebus*, 23c–25a; *Parmenides*, 154–155; Deleuze, 1990, pp. 1–2). In placing them at such a distance from the realm of truth and knowledge, Plato forces such items into the background and treats this lowest realm as some sort of perversion, a deviation from what is true.

Consider, for example, Plato's *Phaedrus* and his treatment of the soul that is far distant from being. Here, Plato gives a ranking of the different bodies a fallen soul would occupy within becoming (248a–e). The soul that has had the poorest vision of being, and fails to resemble being in any way, occupies the lowest body, that of a tyrant, and for Plato, a tyrant is evil. As he maintains in Book IX of the *Republic*: "the man who is shown to be the most evil will also be the most miserable, and the man who is most of a tyrant for the longest time is most and longest miserable" (576b–c). Thus, for Plato, this lowest level of becoming is an evil level.

But the whole notion of truth and knowledge requiring some fixity and permanence is embedded within a view of morality at the heart of Plato's ontology. What is good must be eternal, unchanging, and outside the flux of becoming. What is evil is all that has no relation to the good; all that is constantly shifting and changing. As Dorothea Olkowski remarks: "*[e]vil power, false claimant, perversion, essential turning away*—each of these terms indicates that the process of division is at the basis of what are for Plato moral determinations" (1990, p. 190). For Plato, copies of copies constituted a perverted realm because of their failure to resemble the Forms closely enough. As perversions of reason, they constituted an evil power that had to be rejected. His ultimate motivation was to negate this evil in favor of an eternal and unchanging realm of being where truth and knowledge are found.

My point then is to indicate that the very idea of knowledge requiring some fixity, permanence, purity, and distancing from all that is shifting and changing goes at least as far back as Plato. Going back to Plato, we find that his is not some value-free description of reality and of what can be known, but a value-laden account operating on a morality valuing sameness, fixity, and permanence over all that is shifting, changing, and in constant flux. It is this morality that we find at the heart of Plato's distinctions. But it is also a morality that continues well into present times, finding its expression in various epistemological stances such as that of insight-oriented psychotherapies. Moreover, it is the morality that explains why we do think representationally, for in such thought we fix the flux of existence hoping to make it more manageable, predictable, and calculable. However, there is no reason to accept such a morality and every reason to reject it. As I will indicate shortly, concepts such as those of difference, specificity, uniqueness, change, and flux capture much more faithfully the dynamic nature of the field of experience itself.

Although one can trace insight-oriented psychotherapy's epistemological morality back to Plato, it is the more modern scientific view of knowledge that has had the greatest influence. Guided by scientific methodology as the route to knowledge, insight-oriented psychotherapy adopts an epistemology based on the prevailing scientific ideals of objectivity and value-neutrality. As Lorraine Code comments:

> Implicit in the veneration of objectivity central to *scientific* practice is the conviction that objects of knowledge are separate from knowers and investigators and that they remain separate and unchanged throughout investigative, information-gathering, and knowledge-construction processes. (1991, pp. 31–32)

Indeed, under the scientific view, "[i]f one cannot transcend subjectivity and the particularities of its 'locations,' then there is no knowledge worth analyzing" (Code, 1995, p. 25). In order for what is supposedly discovered to count as knowledge, the particularities of the knower must be transcended so as to maintain the "purity" of the discovery.

But even within the confines of such sciences as physics, let alone psychology, these ideals of purity and value-neutrality do not hold. As feminist, postmodern, and hermeneutic critiques of science have indicated in various and divergent ways, the value neutrality model of science is highly suspect (Babich, 1994; Feyerabend, 1975; Keller and Longino, 1996; Kuhn, 1970; Rouse, 1996). Social and political forces influencing the knower do infiltrate the content as constitutive elements. Under the received understanding of science, "the source of one's hypotheses is epistemically irrelevant" since what matters is the context of justification (Okruhlik, 1992, p. 72). If the hypothesis is tested properly, "then you are justified in holding on to it—whatever its origins" (p. 73). The assumption here of course is that any biases would be filtered out as one tests the hypothesis. However, given that current scientific rationality is "irreducibly comparative" (p. 73)—that is, a choice is made between competing theories—biases are not filtered out. If, for example, we have a choice among three sexist theories explaining gender roles, then whichever theory we decide upon will be sexist. Be as "objective" and as rigorous as you want in testing your theory, you would still end up with a sexist theory! Also, rejecting all three theories does not resolve the issue, for theories are constructed by knowers who are socially and politically situated.

If social and political factors situating the knower do infiltrate a science such as physics, which allegedly is the paradigm of scientific methodology, then it is highly unlikely that insight-oriented psychotherapy can achieve the ideals of its epistemological position. Indeed, it cannot, for such an epistemological position offers the illusion of "seeing everything from nowhere" (Haraway, 1991, p. 189); an understanding that permeates positivist-empiricist thinking and its legacy. In refusing to acknowledge the constitutive role of the knower in the acquisition of knowledge, and hence in its *construction*, insight-oriented psychotherapy is deluding itself by maintaining an impossible detachment from what is known. Its promised ideals of purity and value-neutrality in the so-called discovery of objects are but a denial of the numerous factors situating any knower and which are in turn constitutive in the construction of all knowledge.

Arguing against a disembodied understanding of knowledge, and against "the spell of timelessness, detachment, universality, and absoluteness," Code proposes some subjective factors that do "play a constitutive role in the construction of knowledge" (1991, p. 46). As she maintains:

> Some aspects of subjectivity that play a constitutive role in the construction of knowledge are a subject's (1) historical location; (2) location within specific social and linguistic contexts, which include racial, ethnic, political, class, age, religious, and other identifications; (3) creativity in the construction of knowledge, with the freedoms and responsibilities it entails; and (4) affectivity, commitments, enthusiasms, desires, and interests, in which affectivity contrasts with intellect, or reason in the standard sense. (p. 46)

These factors *situate* a knower and are an integral part of the process by which knowledge is constructed. Contrary to the illusion of a disembodied knower discovering objects in some value-free way, knowledge is a process of construction immanent within a whole web of facts and values. It is situated and local, reflecting a particular perspective within a whole matrix of perspectives. And this should not be understood as the situation of some independent "I," unable to free itself from its particular values, constructing perspectives about some independent object. Indeed, given what I have indicated in chapter two, the notion of such a subject is extremely problematic. As I will explain further in the next section, it is the very subject/object dichotomy itself that I am questioning; aiming to rupture it in such a way that what constitutes an object always depends upon "who" is the knower. As Code remarks, "knowledge is, necessarily and inescapably, the product of an intermingling of subjective and objective elements" (1991, p. 30).

But, some may object, at least some basic knowledge is independent of the knower, as in the claim that this table is rectangular or that cup is blue. Although some knowledge may be intrinsically dependent upon the knower, other more basic claims appear to have no such inextricable relation. Surely such claims are knower independent! While such an objection does seem plausible, it is rooted in the assumption of a world-view whereby some subject experiences an object. Only through such an assumption is such an objection plausible. But even if such an assumption is granted, it is not clear that any basic knowledge claims are independent of the knower. When I look at this table or that cup, I do not observe an object in its totality—namely, from every possible angle—but from a particular perspective determined by my situation with respect to the object. As Sartre (following Edmund Husserl) maintains in the Introduction to *Being and Nothingness* (1943/1956, pp. 5–6), a phenomenon reveals itself to the subject as a series of appearances, of profiles, of which there are an infinite number. But I cannot simultaneously formulate an infinite number of perspectives as if "seeing everything from nowhere." I am limited by my particular position with respect to the object being observed. As such, my pronouncement "this is a blue cup" is knower dependent, for I know the cup only through a finite perspective formed by my particular relation to the cup. If it is a round cup, I do not observe its roundness in its totality at any given moment, but *assume* it from the particular perspective I have on the cup. As a situated knower, I know only through the particular circumstances of my positioning: as these change, so does my knowledge.

In an important passage relating to the nature of knowledge, Friedrich Nietzsche writes:

> Henceforth, my dear philosophers, let us be on guard against the dangerous old conceptual fiction that posited a "pure, will-less, painless, timeless knowing subject"; let us guard against the snares of such contradictory concepts as "pure reason," "absolute spirituality," "knowledge in itself": these always demand that we should think of an eye that is completely unthinkable, an eye turned in no particular direction, in which the active and interpreting forces, through which alone seeing becomes seeing *something*, are supposed to be lacking; they always demand of the eye an absurdity and a nonsense. There is *only* a perspective seeing, *only* a perspective "knowing"; and the *more* affects we allow to speak about one thing, the *more* eyes, different eyes, we can use to observe one thing, the more complete will our "concept" of this thing, our "objectivity," be. (1887/1967, III, 12)

Although this passage contains much more than what I am focusing on at this stage, it is evident that for Nietzsche, as for Code and Donna Haraway, subject-independent knowledge is "an absurdity and a nonsense," demanding "an eye turned in no particular direction." But this is the eye insight-oriented psychotherapy assumes in its epistemological position, and it is the eye clients are subtly influenced to believe in as the way to "health."

Not only does insight-oriented psychotherapy assume an epistemological position where subjective factors particular to the knower are considered irrelevant to the discovery of objects and a potential source of "contamination"; it further assumes that what is supposedly discovered is *represented* to the subject as it really is in itself. As I briefly indicated in chapter two, their conception of subjectivity assumes a representational account of knowledge, where objects are represented to some subject. This account establishes a distinction between the objects and their representations, for no representation is the object itself, but a *re*-presentation of the object to the mind. It is not a presentation of the object since the presentation is the experience of the object itself at the moment of experience, prior to the formation of representations. What the mind captures and records, in other words what it conceptualizes, is a *re*-presentation of the object. This claim immediately raises at least two issues. First, as I indicated in chapter two, are concerns about what is in fact represented, for as the representation is formed, the object has changed. Second, and this stems from the first issue, concerns arise about the relation of the object to the representation. If the representation supposedly constitutes a discovery of the object and is fixed for some period of time at least, how does it relate to what is in constant flux? In other words, if the field of experience is changing, what is the relation that binds any particular representation to any particular "thing"?

Of course, this problem goes back to Plato's view of the relation between what is fixed and what is in flux. For him, the main concern was not with specific examples of beauty or justice, but with "what is beauty?" or "what is justice?" By asking "what is?" Plato established an opposition between essence and appearance leading ultimately to an opposition between being and becoming (Deleuze, 1983, pp. 75–78). His motivation in asking the "what is?" question was to establish being, beyond a realm of apparent becoming. He did not question the reality of becoming or the realm of appearances; he took this order of things as a given and only then asked for the possibility of being given becoming. In his desire to explain being in relation to becoming, he set the two in opposition to each other, in the hope of somehow reconciling them. This separation, however, created a tension between being and becoming, for it conferred upon being a certain exteriority that had to be affirmed simultaneously with the interiority of being in becoming. As the ground for becoming—for what is in constant flux—being had to have a certain connection to becoming: a certain interiority within becoming. Yet, since being was excluded from the realm of space and time, and consequently fixed, it had simultaneously to occupy a certain exteriority to becoming which defined space and time. Thus, Plato was faced with having to affirm both the exteriority and the interiority of being in becoming. Consider, for example, Plato's *Parmenides* 130e–135c in which Parmenides and Socrates discuss the relation of the Forms (being) with individual things (becoming). After a considerable amount of reflection and debate on whether the Forms participate in whole or in part with individual things, Parmenides asks: "Well then, Socrates, how are the other things going to partake of your forms, if they can partake of them neither in part nor as wholes?" To this question Socrates replies: "it seems no easy matter to determine in any way" (131e).

This problem continues to haunt philosophers to the present day. In the guise in which it figures in insight-oriented psychotherapy's epistemological position, it is the problem of explaining how a fixed, or temporarily fixed, representation relates to what is in constant flux. For example, in psychoanalysis, how does a representation of the father relate to the father himself? In other words, insight-oriented psychotherapy's epistemological stance faces a serious problem in trying to explain representational knowledge as the discovery of objects. Since the field of experience, of "objects," is constantly changing, once the representation is formed the object has changed. If this is so, then in what sense is the representation a "discovery," and how does it relate to its object since that object has changed? Even if we do not assume static representations, the question remains as to how any representations relate to objects.

There is also a much more crucial ethical critique of representationalist accounts of knowledge relating to the epistemological-metaphysical critiques I have presented. Although representationalist accounts claim some value-neutrality with respect to their representation of objects, there is an axiological dimension to their position that is reflected in the priority given to unity and identity over difference and multiplicity. And this relates to Plato's moral valuations, as I have indicated. Recall that, for Plato, being as the realm of permanence, fixity, identity, unity, and knowledge was superior to becoming, of which knowledge could not be attained. For him, what reflected unity and identity was valued much more than what was in flux. Similarly, representationalist accounts of knowledge highly value unity and identity, while negating difference and multiplicity, and subsuming them under concepts that unify under the guise of universality and nullify all that is different. I will expand on this point shortly.

Before I elaborate on this critique, it is crucial to indicate what I mean by difference. I do not mean the everyday understanding of the notion, where difference is understood as what distinguishes an object from another: the table differs from the pen which differs from the paper. Here, difference distinguishes one object from another, so that this table is *not* that pen nor is it the paper. It is a negative conception of difference, whereby only the objects themselves have ontological reality and difference is but a placeholder for the negative term in "X is not Y." In the psychotherapeutic context, this understanding of difference operates, for example, within the problem of individuality, which is: "how can the practice of therapy be individualized, and at the same time also be consistent, replicable, or generalized—that is, systematic—across cases" (Held, 1995, p. 15)? In this context, difference is interpreted as individual client "A" not being individual client "B" or individual client "C." And the problem facing psychotherapy is to establish some way to account for the specifics of each individual while being general enough to account for many individuals. But *if* the turn to the application of "postmodern" theory in psychotherapy is motivated by this problem in a desire to reject generalized psychotherapeutic theories, as Barbara Held suggests, then "postmodern" psychotherapists are operating with the negative interpretation of difference. In other words, if "the postmodern narrative therapy movement is in fact a response to the problem of keeping therapy individualized and yet systematic" (Held, 1995, p. 15) then this suggests an understanding of difference as that between individual "A" and "B," which is the negative interpretation of difference. But such an understanding of difference focuses only on two (or more) clients not being the same, and does not recognize or value the difference constituting the client herself or himself, where the client is understood as a constellation of dynamic forces. Put differently, the individual client herself or himself is different from moment to moment and should not be categorized as an identity. To do so already imposes a certain generality onto a specificity. Thus, psychotherapy's problem is not so much how to be individualized and yet remain systematic, but how to account for the positive and real difference constituting any client, and yet remain able to treat the client as a single entity.

When referring to difference then, I am referring to the Nietzschean-Deleuzian understanding of difference, which seeks to recognize the ontological reality of difference, thereby rejecting a merely negative characterization. Under such an understanding, the focus is on the real difference found within the field of experience and within any "object." It is the difference within the moment to moment actualization of an "object" as it occurs within the sensible. If the field of experience is in constant flux, then difference characterizes the moment to moment actualization of any "object," for as soon as an "object" is formed it changes. Under the everyday understanding of difference, the moment to moment actualization of an "object" cannot be captured since it subsumes such actualizations under one unitary concept of the thing. This table at 10:00 is this table at 10:01. Understood in their everyday usage, concepts cannot capture real differences found within the realm of experience. To better understand what I mean by real difference, perhaps we need to think in Kantian terms and return to my account of Immanuel Kant in chapter two. Recall for Kant, a manifold is "given" to the mind and is synthesized into a representation of an object. Over a period of time, different manifolds are repeatedly synthesized as the same object. That is, the table I see now is the same table I saw yesterday. Thus, I cannot distinguish the real difference in each given manifold, for every time the manifold is "given" to me I recognize it as the same table.

With representationalist accounts of knowledge which rely upon unitary concepts to represent objects, it is the everyday understanding of difference that is operative. A representation of "K" differs from a representation of "T" which differs from "W." The real differences within every actualization of "K" cannot be grasped since they are all captured as "K." Thus, the richness of the sensible is lost or subdued in favor of unifying concepts that erase the *experience* of difference and insert an *intelligible* sameness. What is experienced is a rich field in flux; a field of real difference, but it is not recognized as such in representationalist knowledge since the unitary concepts employed to re-present the experience cannot account for the difference. For representationalist accounts of knowledge, their empiricism is not an empiricism that begins with "the concrete richness of the sensible" and remains faithful to this field (Deleuze and Parnet, 1987, p. 54), but an empiricism that seeks to give an account of how the sensible becomes intelligible; seeking to describe how a subject can experience the sensible. As such, representationalist knowledge gives a priority to identity and sameness, subsuming the real difference of the sensible under universal and unitary concepts.

Such a priority to identity results in an epistemological position that values all that is unitary and identical to a high degree, subsuming difference under identity and defining it in everyday understanding as a negative concept. But such a valuation of the unitary and the same over difference is epistemological fascism! If by fascism we understand the tendency to unify and bring together what is divergent and multiple in order for it be subsumed under a unitary label, as for example in political fascism, then representationalist accounts of knowledge amount to a form of fascism. And this constitutes a much more dangerous form of fascism than its political manifestation since it speaks to all that may count as representative knowledge. If our mainstream epistemic practices (representationalist knowledge) are at their very core, so to speak, fascistic, which I am suggesting they are, it should come as no surprise to find fascistic tendencies also at the psychological, political, and ethical levels. Given that representationalist accounts of knowledge are upheld both within and outside the academy, it is hardly surprising that fascistic tendencies have become the norm at many different levels, to the point where they seem "natural," "factual," or "given." For example, consider the "normal" tendency of many who seek the association, friendship, companionship of others who espouse similar values and beliefs—be they political, religious or otherwise. In this familiarity is a certain comfort that overrides differences; subduing them rather than allowing them to proliferate. But this comfort found in familiarity stems from categories of the same rather than difference, indicating a deeply-rooted fascistic tendency. However, there is nothing "natural" about such a tendency since it stems from certain values that reach as far as our epistemological and metaphysical positions. With the concept of desire, for example, Gilles Deleuze and Félix Guattari attempt in *Anti-Oedipus* (1983) to unfold such an epistemological and metaphysical critique to demonstrate the fascism inherent in our understanding of the concept as such. As Michel Foucault comments in the Preface to the work, *Anti-Oedipus* is a book of ethics and an introduction to the non-fascist life. We need not then accept epistemological fascism as the only world-view. In fact, the "situated realism" I present in the next chapter is an attempt to provide a non-fascistic world-view. Nor does a rejection of epistemological fascism necessarily imply a rejection of every political position and every ideology, for political positions and ideologies are maintainable under a different world-view, such as the one I outline in chapter five.

3. Knowledge as Construction

In the preceding sections I have outlined the problematic nature of the epistemological framework clients are absorbed into in insight-oriented psychotherapies. I have suggested that knowledge is a construct of what may be viewed as both "subjective" and "objective" factors, where both the knower and what is known constitute knowledge. Also, in chapter two, I have outlined an alternative account of subjectivity situated within a field of forces such that subjectivity is a certain singularity comprised of a whole multiplicity of forces. It is a mode of individuation immanent within the field of experience. However, this world-view will not be complete without a more detailed unfolding of the metaphysical issues which I consider in the next chapter. In this section, I wish to focus on "the object" of knowledge, outlining an account of knowledge as construction, given the nature of subjectivity as an immanent form of individuation, which I reconsider also in the next chapter.

In many respects, the account I will articulate is in close proximity to Haraway's understanding of situated knowledges (Haraway, 1991). Although Haraway does not explicitly advocate a Nietzschean-Deleuzian account, her views of subjectivity, objectivity, and the construction of knowledge serve as an extremely helpful introduction to the position I wish to articulate. It is through her work, and in particular through her views on situated knowledges and partial perspectives, that I begin this discussion. However, this is not to suggest that other thinkers have not offered similar critiques of representational knowledge. Martin Heidegger, for example, also rejects representational knowledge, arguing for a situated understanding of human beings as beings-in-the-world. What prompts me to associate my position with Haraway rather than Heidegger is the closer proximity to a Nietzschean-Deleuzian world-view I find in Haraway's analysis.

Heidegger's philosophical project, on the other hand, differs in crucial ways from the world-view I advocate in this study and, most importantly, this difference is not entirely dependent on methodology. Although I do not endorse Heidegger's phenomenological approach, it is with the question of being (*Sein*) and its ontological priority in particular that we differ. Those familiar with Heidegger, and his *Being and Time* in particular, would readily admit that his chief concern revolves around the meaning of being (*Sein*) which raises a question that "has today been forgotten" (Heidegger, 1927/1962, p. 21). For Heidegger, Western thought up to and including Nietzsche, has forgotten this most fundamental question and focused instead on the being of entities (the being of beings) rather than on being (*Sein*) itself (Heidegger, 1937–1940/1987, pp. 187–192). Thus, in terms of a starting point, which is perhaps the key point in any philosophical position, the world-view I advocate in this study is at a distance from Heidegger's. As I indicate in chapter two and develop further in chapter five, my starting point is not the question of being (*Sein*), or the being of beings, or even becoming. I simply begin with a given field of experience, a given surface, and only then proceed to articulate certain conceptual tools that do not aim at unfolding the being of beings (or entities), but at developing a certain world-view, a certain perspective that some may choose to live by. It is only after maintaining this initial starting point that I take the first step with Nietzsche and "admit nothing that has being" (Nietzsche, 1967, 708). Contra Heidegger then, being is itself in question within my world-view.

Moreover, and notwithstanding this difference in starting points, which ultimately is based on values as I indicate in the conclusion to this study, Heidegger's position with respect to human beings differs considerably from what I outline in chapter two. Although scholars tend to agree that the "later" Heidegger shifts away from an emphasis on human beings to focus more on being (*Sein*), in *Being and Time* at least, human beings understood as Da-sein (being there or being here) are pivotal in Heidegger's attempt to grasp being (*Sein*). Although contra René Descartes, Heidegger situates Da-sein within the world as already a being-in-the-world; a being-with others and other entities, Da-sein "has a special distinctiveness as compared with other entities" (Heidegger, 1927/1962, p. 32). It is the only entity "in its very Being, that Being is an *issue* for it" (p. 32). Consequently, for Heidegger, Da-sein is "the primary entity to be interrogated" (p. 35) in the quest for the meaning of being (*Sein*) since it "already comports itself, in its Being, towards what we are asking about" (p. 35). Although the situated aspect of Da-sein shares in its situatedness a similarity to the immanent account of subjectivity I present in chapter two, crucial differences exist between the two views. First, unlike Heidegger, I do not claim any "special distinctiveness" with respect to human beings that allows access to a more fundamental question. There is only a singular surface of forces constituting bodies—be they biological, chemical, social, or political. If we are to talk about human beings, then it is in terms of constellations of forces, dynamic and in flux, and constituting personal *identities* across time. Second, and more importantly perhaps, I do not relate becoming back to subjectivity of any type which is contrary to Heidegger's project in *Being and Time*. With Heidegger, being (*Sein*) is related back to Da-sein because of Da-sein's privileged positioning among other entities. Consequently, if the charge of "reductionism" with respect to subjectivity is leveled against my position, then Heidegger is equally reductionistic with respect to the "more fundamental" question of being (*Sein*) which perhaps explains the move away from subjectivity in the "later" Heidegger.

Returning to Haraway, her situated knowledges, partial perspectives, indicate a means to contest disinterested objectivity which posits a disembodied knowing subject with the potential of gaining innocent and pure knowledge. Arguing against the possibility of a disengaged, disembodied, and detached understanding of knowledge, Haraway presents an account of objectivity that aims to be both situated and responsible. As she maintains, "I would like a doctrine of embodied objectivity that accommodates paradoxical and critical feminist science projects: feminist objectivity means quite simply *situated knowledges*" (1991, p. 188). In being situated, objectivity in this sense becomes embodied, locatable, and specific.

Rejecting both positivist-empiricist accounts of innocent objectivity and the "strong social constructionist perspective" (p. 184) for which all talk of objectivity, truth, and knowledge is simply rhetorical, Haraway posits an understanding of objectivity as partial perspective, where the dichotomy between subject and object is ruptured but not totally abolished; maintaining the distinction without maintaining a dichotomy. Her aim is to introduce an understanding of objectivity as a locatable specificity; as a view from somewhere that may therefore demand responsibility. Thus, a space opens for critical construction and deconstruction of knowledges where location and embodiment must be taken into account. It is not an understanding that posits itself dogmatically as the absolute center, but it is what decenters and situates. Yet, as Haraway is quick to indicate, the implication here is not that subjugated positions are preferable because they are somehow innocent, for no such innocent positions exist, but that they are much more likely to be on to, to notice, positions that are "ways of being nowhere while claiming to see comprehensively" (p. 191) where location and embodiment are disregarded in the hope for universality.

Against representationalist accounts of knowledge, Haraway is critical of the view that posits objects somehow out there in the world awaiting discovery (pp. 198–199). In line with her desire to rupture the subject/object dichotomy for the effects it produces, she rejects the logic of discovery that promises an ability to discover the "real," "true," "objective" world if only "we" apply ourselves well enough. The world, according both to Haraway and to me, is not simply out there awaiting discovery. The "object of knowledge" is not considered as discovered, but "as an actor and agent" (p. 198) participating in the construction of knowledge. In this way, Haraway injects into the "object of knowledge" an agency that shifts the production of knowledge from the monological understanding that permeates the logic of discovery, to a dialogical understanding.

Similarly, Haraway rejects accounts of subjectivity that posit some stable and unified "I" divorced from the world and intent on discovering it. For her, subjectivity implies a sense of a self similar to the account I have offered in chapter two: "The knowing self is partial in all its guises, never finished, whole, simply there and original; it is always constructed and stitched together imperfectly, and *therefore* able to join with another" (p. 193). It is a self that is active within a world—multiple, split, contradictory, and in motion. In being fragmentary, multiple and diverse, the self is not immediately known to itself. Echoing Nietzsche's *Genealogy of Morals* where he claims "[w]e are unknown to ourselves, we men of knowledge" (1887/1967, Preface, 1), Haraway maintains "[w]e are not immediately present to ourselves" (1991, p. 192). As such, the self is able to join with another, for it is not an isolated and whole entity capable of being present to itself. It is situated not just in the world, but in relation to other subjects.

While it is tempting to see in Haraway, as indeed in the account I have been unfolding, a move towards some form of "antirealism," this reading would constitute a serious mistake, for to maintain knowledge as a construction in no way entails a move towards "antirealism." In a lengthy and important footnote to her 1997 book *Modest_Witness*, Haraway explicitly addresses this issue, rejecting the label "antirealism."

> It is important that my account of reality as an effect of an observing interaction, as opposed to a treasure awaiting discovery, not be misunderstood. "Reality" is certainly not "made up" in scientific practice, but it is collectively, materially, and semiotically constructed—that is, put together, made to cohere, worked up for and by us in some ways and not others. This is not a relativist position, if by relativism one means that the facts and models, including mathematical models, of natural scientific accounts of the world are merely matters of desire, opinion, speculation, fantasy, or any other such "mental" faculty. (pp. 301–302)

Thus, reality for Haraway is a material-semiotic construct; an interim product of interactive relationships between forces, empirically grounded without being observer-independent. This view is similar to the position I advocate in chapter two in terms of forces. It refers to the production of worlds that are not based on mere desire, opinion or fantasy, "but worlds that must be lived in consequence in some ways and not others" (pp. 301–302).

While I am in agreement with Haraway on the nature of this production and with the world-view she articulates, there remains the crucial question of locating this production in relation to the field of experience. If subjectivity is understood as a form of individuation immanent within a field in flux and articulated in terms of forces, as I have indicated briefly in chapter two, then how is production accounted for within such a field? In order to reply to this question and to understand better the position I will unfold, it is helpful to consider first the relation between David Hume and Kant since the route I advocate combines elements of their philosophies.

Recall that, for Hume, the basic epistemological distinction was between impressions and ideas. Experience provides impressions out of which ideas or representations are generated. For him, all knowledge is ultimately derived from experience; from the impressions received. In Hume, no Kantian categories modify the given, nor is there any notion of a principle of unification similar to Kant's transcendental apperception. Indeed, for Hume, there is no subject similar to the Kantian transcendental "I" required for the possibility of experience. Looking inside himself, Hume could not find any simple "I" to be labeled as such.

> For my part, when I enter most intimately into what I call *myself*, I always stumble on some particular perception or other, of heat or cold, light or shade. . . . I never can catch *myself* at any time without a perception, and never can observe any thing but the perception. . . . If any one upon serious and unprejudic'd reflexion, thinks he has a different notion of *himself*, I must confess I can reason no longer with him. (1739–1740/1978, p. 252)

Unlike Kant and his network model of experience as an a priori network of categories and transcendental apperception, Hume does not postulate the mind's participation in the initial acquisition of knowledge. The mind passively receives impressions which putatively correspond to objects. Although for Hume the mind can imaginatively construct ideas from what was received, the initial receptivity of impressions is passive, and does not require some a priori network to modify the given. It is Kant who insists upon the production involved in all knowledge. However, for Kant such a production *must* be the result of an a priori network of categories and transcendental apperception: a network that imposes upon the manifold a whole framework that in turn allows for the possibility of representations. For Kant, representations are not simply given to the mind, but must first be generated in a *synthesis* before the mind is capable of being aware of any such representations. Thus, the mind has certain a priori abilities that allow for the possibility of knowledge. Among these abilities is the mind's power to unify objects in one experience. And this unity of representations is ultimately the "I" Hume was searching for through introspection.

But there is another route to be taken combining Hume's empiricism and Kant's synthesis, while rejecting Hume's psychological model of passive receptivity and Kant's insistence on locating the synthesis in an a priori subject. It is a route that relies both on empirical reality as a material field and on the production involved in knowledge(s), without relegating this production to anything like a unified Kantian "I." This is the route I believe Nietzsche, Deleuze, and Haraway take through removing the synthesis from the subject and placing it within the field of experience as an immanent productivity. Contrary to Hume and Kant whose starting points assume a representationalist epistemology—that is, they begin by assuming we know through representations—under this different route, the starting point is the field of experience itself—the empirical world—asking how "subject" and "object" are constituted within this field. And the answer is they are constructed through a synthesis immanent within experience as constellations of forces in certain relations.

The synthesis as "webbed connections" (Haraway, 1991, p. 191) is the production of reality as a material-semiotic construct wherein the "subject" and "object" are constructed, albeit partially and continuously. They are constructed as a relation of forces immanent within experience and in relation to other forces. "Subject" and "object," although individuated, remain as relations of forces constructed through an immanent synthesis, which is no longer a synthesis of a unified and closed subject. Given the open and dynamic nature of experience, production remains always partial, incomplete, and in flux. What guides this relation of forces, this synthesis, are power, interpretation, and valuation, which I will discuss in the next chapter. For the present, I wish only to emphasize the crucial point of removing production out of a unified "I" and placing it within the field of experience. In this way, both "subject" and "object" are constructs determined through specific, situated relations of forces.

Although it is in the following chapter that I consider the practical implications of such an understanding of "subject" and "object," at least two tentative conclusions may be made at this stage regarding psychotherapeutic practice. First, contrary to the claim that the psychotherapeutic process assists in the "discovery" of "facts" about the client that exist independent of any particular theoretical orientation, any knowledge attained during the course of therapy results from a construction involving both "subjective" and "objective" factors. Through the configuration and reconfiguration of various force relations, knowledge is constructed as a certain synthesis of forces in certain relations. And these forces include "subjective" factors situating both the client and the therapist. Indeed, echoing Code that "objectivity requires taking subjectivity into account" (1991, p. 31), such "subjective" factors are required for objectivity. Second, the subject of knowledge is not some "I" that "discovers" "facts" in some value-neutral way, but is itself a construct of various force relations immanent within the very fabric it seeks to know. Consequently, it is not a question of "discovering" some "true" or "core" self, but of constructing, configuring, and reconfiguring various singularities that remain partial, incomplete, and in flux.

Finally, with regard to knowledge as construction, it is tempting to view the position I have been advocating, with its emphasis on situatedness, perspective, and production, as somehow "relativist" and therefore susceptible to the charge of self-referential inconsistency. Typically, this charge may be posed in the form of the question: If all knowledge is situated, embodied, local, and perspectival, then is this claim itself situated or not? If it is not itself situated then clearly it is not true that all knowledge is situated, for there is at least one claim, namely the claim itself, which is not situated. If, on the other hand, the claim is itself situated, then it cannot be about all knowledge. It cannot be a universal claim. Thus, in either case, there is a problem of self-reference.

In her essay, "Must a Feminist Be a Relativist After All?" Code indicates how this charge is typically brought against "relativists" and used as a means of rejecting "relativism" (1995, pp. 185–207). Against it, Code argues that no committed and honest "relativist" would deny the locatedness of her thesis (p. 197). However, this does not imply the thesis is self-refuting, for the charge itself

> begs the very question that relativists are engaged in addressing, especially in its assumption that there *are* absolute, timeless, dislocated, pre-supposition-free truths. Having examined the evidence to the best of her/his ability, a relativist concludes that there can be no context-free truth: neither the relativist thesis itself, nor any other. (p. 197)

In such a charge against "relativism," Code argues that "relativists" are wrongly addressed from within a "metaphysic" that assumes absolute, universal "truths" (p. 198). On this view, to charge the position I have been advocating with self-referential inconsistency is to fail to recognize the different metaphysical world-view in which knowledge as construction is situated. It would be a mistake founded upon judging an epistemic thesis from the wrong metaphysic. However, it would be an understandable mistake since it is in the next chapter that I consider the details of the world-view I have been advocating. I will return to this issue in chapter five.

From the standard view of insight-oriented psychotherapies, and from the assumptions such therapies make about the nature of the self, it is evident that their epistemological stance is characterized by an appeal to the "discovery" of "facts," which are independent of the particular theoretical and methodological tools applied. Knowledge, according to such therapies, is the "discovery" of certain preexisting facts that the psychotherapeutic process assists in unveiling and understanding. But, as I have attempted to show, such an understanding of knowledge is extremely problematic, since it is based upon a denial of the various forces—be they social, political, economic, or otherwise—situating any knower and constitutive of all that is known.

Consequently, knowledge claims are not solely a matter of discovery, but construction. Moreover, this denial is rooted in a certain valuation that places a much higher degree of value on categories of sameness than on those which seek difference and multiplicity. Thus, insight-oriented psychotherapists are not only deceiving their clients by promising them "discovery" when such a discovery is not possible, but they are also constructing them along preconceived valuations rooted in a fascistic tendency to deny real difference. Unless one values this fascistic tendency over and above what is counter to it, insight-oriented psychotherapies are problematic. They are problematic because of the values they endorse.

Five

METAPHYSICAL ISSUES

1. Two Versions of Realism

The philosophical framework or world-view clients are absorbed into during the course of therapy is not only epistemologically questionable, as I indicate in the previous chapter, but relies also on a problematic metaphysical stance. This is perhaps even more worrisome since one's metaphysical position or world-view plays a crucial role in the attitudes, beliefs, and values adopted. In viewing the world in certain ways and not others, one becomes more disposed to accepting particular attitudes, beliefs, and values over others. For many, however, who are not engaged in philosophical reflection, their particular world-view or metaphysical assumptions are perhaps unconscious; conditioned by religious, social, and familial factors. Nevertheless, unconscious as it may be, their underlying metaphysical stance plays a crucial role in their relation to the world and other people. As such, the metaphysical dimension of the philosophical framework clients are absorbed into during the course of therapy is of crucial importance.

But if it is exceedingly difficult to find a clear articulation of the epistemological assumptions made by insight-oriented psychotherapists, it is even more difficult to find their metaphysical assumptions, particularly as they relate to their understanding of "realism." In the previous chapter, I indicated that insight-oriented psychotherapy's epistemological assumptions become evident from the standard view presented in chapter one and from the assumptions such therapies make about the nature of subjectivity, as I have presented it in chapter two. However, with respect to their metaphysical stance, the case differs since from their epistemological assumptions a whole variety of differing metaphysical positions may be inferred, complicating matters considerably.

Yet, by considering the most crucial components of insight-oriented psychotherapy's epistemological position, it is still possible to articulate some understanding at least of its metaphysical position. I say "some understanding" because even though most, if not all, epistemological positions assume a certain metaphysics, the relation between the two is not of a simple one-to-one correspondence. For example, as I will argue at a later stage, it is quite possible to maintain knowledge as construction while upholding a "realist" metaphysics. Put differently, an epistemic thesis maintaining knowledge as construction does not necessarily assume an "antirealist" metaphysical position.

Recall from chapter four the most significant characteristics of insight-oriented psychotherapy's understanding of knowledge. To know "p" is the case is to have some "S" *discover* this *fact* in such a way that the personal characteristics of "S" do not influence the discovery of "p." As a discoverable fact, "p" is independent of "S" and uncontaminated by it, if "p" is known objectively. As a discoverable fact, "p" may be known by any "S" given the right circumstances, and is not dependent upon any "S" for its discovery. This suggests that "p's" reality, so to speak, is independent of "S" implying quite clearly, I believe, a "realist" metaphysical stance. For me to know objects in the world, I need to discover them directly, without allowing any of my personal characteristics to contaminate or influence such discovery.

However, although from insight-oriented psychotherapy's epistemological position it is quite evident that they assume a "realist" metaphysics, it is not at all clear what is meant by such "realism" since several versions are possible, two of which I consider below. What is clear is that their understanding of "realism" must take into account and explain their epistemological position. It must be a form of "realism" whereby objects are discovered rather than constructed. But before turning to two possible versions of "realism" that may further reveal insight-oriented psychotherapy's metaphysical stance, it is important to detour slightly and briefly consider the definitions of realism and antirealism.

The whole realist/antirealist debate within the philosophical tradition is a complex and arduous debate not easily untangled. Nevertheless, certain generalizations about the two positions are possible, vague and unclear as they may be. Focusing on realism initially, the more accessible characterization of the doctrine "states that the knower can attain knowledge of an independent reality—that is, reality that is objective in the sense that it does not originate in the knower, or knowing subject" (Held, 1995, p. 4). And as Barbara Held further explains, "independent reality" refers to a separation between the knower and what is known such that what is known is known directly as it is in itself (pp. 4–5). Such a characterization of realism clearly depends upon a particular epistemological view—namely, that at least some objects of knowledge are directly accessible by the knower. But although we may accept such a characterization as a particular version of realism, we need not accept it as a universal characterization that rules out any other possible version.

As I indicate in chapter four in reference to Donna Haraway, realism may also be characterized as a doctrine which recognizes empirical reality as an integral contributor to the production of knowledge; constraining and restricting the production of knowledge in such a way that what is known cannot be based on mere desire, opinion or fantasy. In this sense, realism is not restricted to any particular epistemological stance, but to whether some material reality restricts and constrains knowers in some ways and not others.

Perhaps a useful way to consider such a characterization of realism is to view it as the more general type wherein one can identify particular versions, as those identified by Held, for example. In either case, the crucial point is that a realist doctrine need not depend upon understanding knowledge as either discovery or construction.

But if realism is not dependent upon a characterization of knowledge that demands direct access to the thing as it is in itself, then Held's characterization of antirealism must be rejected. According to Held, for antirealists

> a theory, language, construct, or narrative always intervenes, or mediates, between the knower and the known—that is, between the knower and the targeted independent reality that is usually presumed to exist. Therefore, the knower can never have direct awareness of an independent (of the knower) reality. (1995, p. 7)

Clearly, however, given the more general characterization of realism I indicate, the inability of a knower to have direct access to what is known need not imply antirealism. The implication would apply only if Held's characterization of realism were taken as the only feasible version of realism, which in my view is not the case. Also, it would be a mistake to consider Held's characterization of antirealism as a description of the metaphysical position I have been advocating in previous chapters and will expand upon below. As I have suggested and will indicate further at a later stage, because the worldview I am advocating does not rely on strict distinctions between the knower and what is known, it rejects any reference to an "independent reality." Antirealism, then, may be characterized as a doctrine that rejects the view that an empirical reality constrains us in some ways and not others. As such, for a strict antirealist, no material reality limits us in any way. This is similar to the position Held characterizes as radical antirealism which rejects "the existence of any mind-independent reality" (1995, p. 257).

Of course, there are many complexities to the realist/antirealist debate which I have not touched upon. My main concern in this chapter is to outline two possible versions of realism that may situate insight-oriented psychotherapy's metaphysical stance, and to indicate a third version that does not rely on knowledge as discovery. What, then, are the two versions that may capture insight-oriented psychotherapy's metaphysical stance? And are both problematic, leading to the conclusion that clients are not only absorbed into the therapist's philosophical framework, but they are also absorbed into an epistemologically and metaphysically questionable framework?

Held's definition of realism captures the two versions I wish to unfold. The first, which is a kind of generic, naive, or commonsensical realism, suggests the traditional epistemological-metaphysical thesis that knowers have direct access to an independent reality whose true nature is discoverable irrespective of any particular knower. Thus, it is possible to discover the nature of reality as it is in itself, and to test the truthfulness of knowledge claims by their correspondence with reality. Given insight-oriented psychotherapy's epistemological stance, this form of realism would allow for claims maintaining that certain facts or truths about the client's psychological makeup and past are discoverable through therapy. Through the application of a specific theory and method, and through the use of correct interpretations, the client's true psychological makeup and history can be laid open and known.

This version of realism, in many respects, is Humean in its denial of the knower's participation in knowledge. For David Hume, the mind passively receives impressions out of which it generates representations or ideas, and all knowledge is ultimately derived from such impressions. Although for Hume the mind can imaginatively construct ideas from what was received, the initial receptivity of impressions is passive, and does not require some a priori network to modify the given. However, as Immanuel Kant, Friedrich Nietzsche, Gilles Deleuze, Michel Foucault, Lorraine Code, Haraway, and many other philosophers since have maintained, knowers are not passive receptors of an independent reality, but are active participants in the production of knowledge. As indicated previously, with Kant, for example, and his network of categories and transcendental apperception, representations are not simply given to the mind, but must be generated through a synthesis before any awareness of them is possible. Knowledge, therefore, is at the very least not achieved in passive receptivity of a reality as it is in itself. It is the product of a synthesis initiated by the knower, through which knowledge is possible.

This version of realism, which Held rightly rejects, is truly naive in believing that the contribution of a knower is not epistemologically significant (Code, 1981). Whether one agrees with the details of Kant's position is irrelevant here since the crucial issue revolves around whether knowledge is discovered or constructed, rather than how it is constructed. If, as Kant and others have claimed, a knower is actively involved in the production of knowledge, and if we recognize what Kant did not, that a knower is always situated within certain social, historical, political, linguistic, and other contexts, then the notion of passively discovering reality becomes extremely implausible. Indeed, within the psychotherapeutic context, given the variety of forces that permeate the therapeutic encounter, which I outlined in chapter three, and the problematic nature of insight-oriented psychotherapy's epistemological stance, a discovery of the client's psychological makeup and past in the naive realist sense is highly implausible.

However, as Held suggests in *Back to Reality: A Critique of Postmodern Theory in Psychotherapy*, the naive realist version of realism is not the only version available for insight-oriented psychotherapies. Relying on Edward Pols's (1992, 1998) thesis of "radical realism," Held advocates a "modest realism" in therapy that relies upon a more sophisticated and complex version of naive realism. Perhaps then, this second version of realism may adequately describe insight-oriented psychotherapy's metaphysical stance. As such, we need to consider it in order not to be accused of concluding too hastily that insight-oriented psychotherapy assumes a questionable metaphysical position. Since this second version of realism is more complex than the first, I would like to begin by simply elaborating the position as clearly as possible. Following that, I will consider a brief application of it to psychotherapy. Although I find much that is of concern in Pols's position, I will refrain from commenting on it until a later stage.

For Pols, a primary concern is explaining how rationality (understood as a faculty we possess) provides us with direct knowledge of being, or the real, without *making* the real in any sense (1992, p. 153). That is, he wishes to explain how at least some of our knowledge is a result of direct access to objects as they are in themselves. For this purpose, he identifies two functions of rationality through which knowledge is possible: rational awareness and the formative function (p. 122). The formative function of rationality is what "makes not ex nihilo but rather out of what is available to it by virtue of rational awareness" (p. 145). This includes such artifacts as houses and works of art, and propositional claims about the nature of reality derived from "our rational awareness of the nonpropositional" (p. 146). As Held explains, the formative function "creates, makes, constitutes, or constructs things like art, houses, music, and . . . (linguistic) propositions—or theories/stories/narratives—about life and about the world in general" (1995, pp. 163–164).

For Pols, what allows us to have direct access to the real, or being, is rational awareness in its two modes. The primary mode of rational awareness constitutes the beginning of all knowledge, since it is our direct awareness of temporospatial things such as birds, trees, or chairs (1992, pp. 126–127). And as Held maintains, "[t]hese entities and events are in no sense formed, constructed, or constituted by the formative function" (1995, p. 164). The secondary mode of rational awareness is direct awareness of things that are not temporospatial, such as propositions and other primarily linguistic items (Pols, 1992, pp. 136–138). As Held explains, "the fact that we can form or constitute linguistic items does not mean that being rationally aware of linguistic items is itself a formative or constitutive act" (1995, p. 165). Although the formative function plays a crucial role in Pols's overall stance, his articulation of the primary and secondary modes of rational awareness remains crucial to understanding the nature of his "radical realism." Since the secondary mode is secondary only in the sense of distinguishing the items of which we are directly aware—whether or not they are temporospatial—we may, for simplicity, focus upon the primary mode of rational awareness to further unravel his version of "radical realism."

As indicated, the primary mode of rational awareness allows for direct knowledge of objects such as birds, trees, or chairs. It is "direct" in the sense that it is "not known by way of theory or by way of other linguistic entities that are attended to by the knower" (Held, 1995, p. 165). As Pols claims, items such as

> impressions, ideas, concepts, or universals . . . do not, by virtue of some privileged direct access to them on our part, mediate our rational-experiential engagement with temporospatial things and accordingly make that engagement indirect and philosophically problematic. If we can in fact become rationally aware of such items, that awareness follows upon and does not precede our rational awareness of temporospatial things. (1992, p. 130)

Also, our direct rational awareness is active rather than passive, as it is in the naive realist view, in the sense that it has "both a rational and an empirical, or experiential, pole" where "the two poles are inseparably fused and in mutual support, even though each is distinguishable and partly characterizable" (Pols, 1992, p. 155). As such, "[k]nowing is, before all other things, an activity, function, state, or condition of the knower that completes itself in the independently real" (p. 155).

According to Pols, it would be a mistake to analyze direct rational awareness through splitting the activity into discrete components: the rational and the empirical (1998, pp. 103–104). Typically, for Pols, the rational component is then identified as "concepts, ideas, categories, representations, terms, and propositions" while the empirical aspect is identified as "sensory experience, and . . . categorized as impressions, sensations, perceptions, feelings, and the like" (p. 103). Having made such a split, epistemologists, according to Pols, then attempt to claim "that the process of knowing concrete things like lilacs . . . only begins with such in-the-mind things, the concrete things being indirectly known (inferred) by mind, believed in by mind, postulated by mind" (p. 103). Similarly, it would be a mistake to understand direct rational awareness as representational in character, for "representation plays no role whatsoever" in it (p. 109). Although representations are important to us, for Pols, they are of no use "if we cannot know some things that are not in any sense representations" (p. 109).

In short, Pols's version of realism may be summarized as a more restricted form of the broader version of realism I presented initially. It is more restricted in that it does not claim all of our knowledge results from direct access to "reality" as it is in itself, but only some. In other words, in some instances, we can discover reality as it is in itself. When we do not have direct access to reality as it is in itself, we can approximate reality through theories, for example, that rely on what is available through direct access. In other words, through theories we can extend the knowledge gained through direct access to reality. But there are important differences between the two versions of realism I have presented. For Pols, direct rational awareness is active and not passive as in naive realism, and in it the two poles (rational and experiential) are "inseparably fused and in mutual support, even though each is distinguishable and partly characterizable" (Pols, 1992, p. 155). Clearly then, Pols's position is at odds with the epistemological account I advocate in chapter four where all knowledge is viewed as construction.

Although Pols does not concern himself with psychotherapy in *Radical Realism* and *Mind Regained*, it is useful to consider briefly the application of his "radical realism" to psychotherapy. Since Held endorses his position, consider the following example she provides:

> [T]he therapist can have direct (i.e. unmediated by theory) awareness of a client pacing during a session, waving her arms about, and uttering sentences about how agitated she feels. These sentences may or may not tell the therapist something true about the client's psychological state, which the therapist cannot observe directly. But based on what he has observed directly and on his knowledge of psychological principles, the therapist can nonetheless develop, or construct, a theory about what is causing that behavior, what the client's intent in so behaving is, and so forth. (1995, p. 6)

Put differently, if Pols's claims hold, then the therapist can discover at least some things about the client—namely, that she is pacing, waving her arms, and uttering sentences. Although such knowledge is not infallible, if it is discovered accurately, the therapist can employ his knowledge of psychological principles to develop a theory explaining her behavior. Relying on what is *directly* observed, the therapist *constructs* a theory about what is causing the behavior, what it means, and so forth. As such, not all knowledge is construction, for at least "some aspects" of the client are directly discoverable by the therapist.

But, we may ask, what are these aspects that are directly discoverable? Do they include "facts" about the client's life history or psychological make-up? If Pols's version of realism is to account for insight-oriented psychotherapy's metaphysical stance, then it needs to be a realism that accounts for its epistemological stance also. That is, it must be a realism that accounts for the discovery of "facts" about a client's personality, behaviors, and psychological make-up. However, from the example, it is evident that what is directly discovered only includes certain actions and behaviors observed during therapy. Consequently, if Pols's version of realism is to account for insight-oriented psychotherapy's metaphysical stance, it accounts for it in an extremely minimal way, since such therapies claim to discover much more than what Pols's position allows for. In other words, even if we accept Pols's realism, it does not appear to be an adequate metaphysical foundation for the epistemic requirements of insight-oriented psychotherapy.

Nonetheless, some may object at this stage by questioning my account of insight-oriented psychotherapy's epistemological claims, arguing perhaps that I overstate what such therapies claim to discover during therapy. Consequently, had I presented insight-oriented psychotherapy's epistemological claims differently, or in such a manner that they conform to Held's example—only claiming the discovery of what is directly observed in therapy—then Pols's version of realism may serve as an adequate metaphysical foundation. Although I do not believe to have overstated insight-oriented psychotherapy's epistemological claims, this possible objection assumes the acceptability of Pols's "radical realism." However, this is hardly the case. Focusing initially on the more general aspect of Pols's position, it becomes apparent that Pols *assumes* the world-view in which he situates what appears to be for him the problem. In other words, he assumes a certain metaphysical outlook within which he poses a certain question and then proceeds to answer it. However, there is no reason why his particular outlook should be accepted as the universally "true" or "correct" metaphysics. Indeed, what is in question is the very outlook he assumes, and the metaphysical assumptions he makes. More specifically, Pols assumes "independent reality," "being," "the real," rationality as one of our faculties, and proceeds to pose the question he wishes to consider within the parameters of these notions, assuming that such notions actually make sense, and are readily accepted by all! This, however, needs further clarification.

Consider, for example, the opening pages of Pols's *Radical Realism*.

> This book is about the nature and scope of rationality, more precisely, about its capacity to know reality: to know whatever in particulars and in the general nature of things is independent of our minds—whatever is in no sense dependent on any formative, or productive, powers rationality may also have. (1992, p. 1)

This opening sentence clearly suggests a world-view which assumes on the one hand individuals with "minds" and a capacity to be "rational," and on the other a "reality" with "particulars." Within this assumed world-view, Pols proceeds to ask:

> How then do *we* set about answering the original question? It is a question about the real (that in particulars and in the general nature of

things which the human mind has in no sense made); but it is also about the human mind and its capacities and limitations. (p. 20)

Clearly, the very nature of his question assumes a world-view, a starting point, in a world of particulars on the one hand, and of human minds on the other. But these very assumptions are themselves questionable! It is not at all evident that reference to an "independent reality" or a world of particulars or a human mind is readily acceptable. Such notions, considered from the perspective of another world-view such as the one I have been advocating throughout this study, actually do not make any sense. It is only by initially accepting Pols's world-view—that is, assuming it—that such notions can be posited and a certain problematic posed.

The point I am attempting to make is difficult to articulate without further discussion of such terms as "metaphysics" and "world-view" which I consider at a later stage. Nevertheless, given Pols's various remarks, it is fairly evident that he assumes a certain outlook from the very beginning of his project; an outlook which we need not readily accept. This assumption is further evidenced by the manner in which he defines realism and antirealism. For Pols, a claim that denies any direct access whatsoever to some "independent reality" expresses an antirealist position. Conversely, a realist stance, according to Pols, must allow for at least some direct access to objects in themselves, without such access being mediated by theory or language (1992, pp. 5–9). In other words, Pols's definition of realism and antirealism is the definition I outlined earlier as the more accessible characterization. And clearly, such a definition already assumes a certain world-view, a certain outlook, rejecting the possibility of any other version of realism.

Pols, however, is likely to object to my criticism by noting that he does not assume any world-view, but addresses an issue arising from our own experience of the world. For example, looking around this room I see a desk. Am I not entitled to inquire whether I am directly aware of this desk or whether my knowledge of it is mediated in some way? And from such epistemological considerations, the realist/antirealist debate is formulated in terms that inquire about the possibility of gaining direct (unmediated) awareness of objects in themselves. After all, Pols may add, "the production of a sound metaphysics requires an adequate epistemological correlative. That in turn requires an *attention to* our own rational capacity rather than the production of one more *theory about it* . . . ." (1992, p. 24).

For Pols, my introduction of a third possible version of realism within which knowledge is constructed rather than discovered would perhaps indicate a resistance on my part to accepting my position as antirealist. Since Pols does not view his initial starting point as an assumption, but as what experience calls for, he cannot accept any other possibility. But this is my point exactly! In carving-up the world in a certain way and not another, and in basing such an outlook on what experience supposedly imposes, Pols is unable to accept any other version of realism, since that would undermine his very project. To accept the possibility of some other perspective would not only imply that his position is itself a perspective, but that the notions advocated by his position—mind, rationality, being, particular objects—are themselves questionable, at the very least. Consequently, I do not expect Pols to accept the perspectival nature of his overall position, and that it is itself a situated claim.

But even if we grant Pols his initial assumption of a particular worldview, there remains the questionable nature of "direct rational awareness" itself. According to Pols, what allows for direct access to objects as they are in themselves is direct rational awareness which is an inseparable "fusion" of two poles—the rational and experiential. This fusion, according to Pols, which is a function of our rationality, does not require justification by way of theories or the making of constructs, but is recognized by our attending to rational awareness and its "naturally reflexive function" (1992, p. 35). In "cultivating and enhancing the reflexive component" of rational awareness, I am able to recognize my "cognitive attainment" of the desk before me as the "realization, or actualization, of rational awareness." That is, I am able to recognize the inseparable fusion of my rational pole with the experiential pole (p. 34).

Yet, when I do attend to this desk before me, the only "reflexive epiphany" (Pols, 1992, p. 34) I am aware of is the perspectival nature of my experience. As I indicated in chapter four with reference to Jean-Paul Sartre, when I do attend to this desk before me, I do not and cannot attend to it from every possible angle, but only from a perspective determined by my situation with respect to the object. As a finite being I am limited by my particular temporal and spatial positioning and cannot possibly experience the desk from an infinite number of perspectives. My pronouncement "this is a desk before me" depends upon a finite perspective formed by my particular relation to the desk. If it is rectangular, I do not observe its shape in totality at any given moment, but *assume* it from the particular finite perspective I have on the desk. As a situated knower, I know only through the particular finite circumstances of my positioning: as these change, so does my knowledge. Consequently, I contribute to my knowledge of the desk and construct it in certain ways and not others. Pols's remarks then, that he need not prove the fusion of the rational and experiential, "but merely call attention to it in an appropriate way" seem suspect (1992, p. 3). I can equally call attention to the perspectival nature of our experience and claim that it needs no proof but appropriate attention only. Of course, this does not indicate Pols is wrong, but one cannot know through "appropriate attention" which is the correct account.

Furthermore, although Pols does claim that the rational pole does not make or construct the object in any sense, he cannot know that. For Pols, the rational pole, although fused with the experiential pole in direct rational awareness, does not make or construct the object in any way. That is, even though our direct knowledge of objects is active and not passive, this activity does not imply that the object is constructed in any way. But how does Pols know that? Simply attending "reflexively [to] the functions of mind as they *are"* (Pols, 1998, p. 111) does not imply that the rational pole is not making or constructing the object in any way. To establish that, Pols must somehow be able to step out himself and observe himself while the two poles are fusing! This inability for a god-like perspective is a crucial point made by Kant and often omitted in any discussion of his epistemology, including Pols's account of Kant.

For Kant, the distinction between appearances and things in themselves is not meant to suggest a two world scenario—the one we experience and the one somehow existing outside our field of experience. His interest in making the distinction is to demonstrate the mind's participation in the production of knowledge; to indicate the impossibility of our knowing any thing as it is in itself, for to know a thing the mind must participate actively in the production of such knowledge. Things as they are in themselves do play a role in our knowledge by the manner in which they affect us, though *we can never know whether we have accessed such things as they are in themselves.* As such, the thing in itself is for Kant a limiting notion. It limits what we can claim about the nature of our knowledge (Kant, 1787/1933, A256). And this is the crucial point that Pols fails to gain from Kant's epistemology, even though he is right to distance himself from the Kantian epistemological position.

Naturally, Pols would object to my critique arguing, perhaps, that I am not attending in an appropriate manner to what our mind does, and am, therefore, unable to accept his account of fusion. If only I applied myself appropriately, I would realize the inevitability of direct rational awareness. But what does proper or appropriate attention mean? Implicitly, under Pols's account, appropriate attention corresponds with an acceptance of his initial starting point, which assumes the notions I indicated earlier, and from which he unfolds his account. Put differently, we must begin by accepting such notions as "real," or "being," or "rationality," as somehow self-evident, perhaps through commonsense. But this is hardly acceptable, for these notions and the world-view they portray is itself in question.

Ultimately, the problematic nature of Pols's position rests upon him not acknowledging that his starting point already assumes a world-view, and is consequently a particular perspective among others, not a universal truth about the nature of knowledge. Although he is quite correct in distancing himself from Kant's epistemological stance, he shares with Kant a similar starting point in that both begin by asking a similar question: Given that we do have experience of objects, how is this possible? But this question already assumes a certain world-view in its reference to "we" and "objects." It assumes a certain dichotomy between subject and object that is itself in question.

If Pols's account, then, rests upon a questionable starting point, in possibly accounting for insight-oriented psychotherapy's epistemological stance, it is problematic. Moreover, even if we accept the details of his account, the mere fact that it relies on an assumed starting point is of ethical concern, with respect to psychotherapy. From an ethical standpoint, why should clients be absorbed into a metaphysical stance that assumes a certain world-view and posits it as the universally "true" or "correct" view? Consequently, both versions of realism I have considered are not adequate to account for insight-oriented psychotherapy's epistemological position.

2. Situated Realism

Given the stance I have been advocating throughout this study, especially regarding the nature of subjectivity and knowledge, it is tempting to conclude that I am advocating an antirealist position. But this is not the case. The position I have been advocating, which in this section I unfold in greater detail, can only be considered antirealist if one is to assume "the discovery of objects as they are in themselves" is a necessary component of realism. And, as I have suggested, there is no reason to make such an assumption unless one also assumes a certain world-view. If we are to remain realists then, without assuming a world of subjects discovering independent objects, how is such a realism possible? Put differently, what other version of realism is possible if we reject the two versions I indicated earlier? This is the main focus of this section.

Before engaging and explicating what I call "situated realism," it is crucial to consider, albeit briefly, such terms as "metaphysics," "ontology," and "world-view." Although these terms have a long and complex history, it is important to note that the "situated realism" I elaborate is not posited as traditional metaphysics or ontology, but as a certain perspective; a certain world-view. In general terms, metaphysics is characterized as an attempt to provide a universal description of reality as a whole, where the subject positing the account is incorporated into the description. But, as Ruediger Grimm has suggested (1979, pp. 289–292), metaphysical accounts are inevitably circular, for in advancing claims about reality as a whole, the claim itself must either be part of the account or be external to it. If it is part of the account then it must explain itself as part of the account, which is not possible since a claim about reality as a whole has no other ground to explain itself. If it is external to the account, then the account is clearly not about reality as a whole, for there is at least one claim—namely, the claim itself—that is not part of it. In either case, metaphysical views are caught in this self-referential web. With ontology, which is perhaps part of metaphysics, the term is more ambiguous in that it offers a theory of being. But "being" is itself questionable in the view I explicate and so it would be a mistake to understand "situated realism" as a theory of being. In a general sense, "situated realism" is best understood as a certain world-view; a certain perspective that entails a particular way of thinking and living. It is a way of life that conceives of reality in a certain way while simultaneously realizing the situated nature of the description, allowing for the possibility of other views. This will become clearer as I unfold the position, but it is important to realize at this initial stage that I am not advocating a metaphysics or ontology understood in the senses just described.

The world-view I am attempting to explicate, and whose key elements I introduced in previous chapters, takes its starting point from the field of experience. In other words, the starting point is reality in its totality as a certain surface, plane, or field that is experienced. But this must not be understood in a commonsensical way as a surface of "subjects" and "objects" wherein "subjects" experience "objects." It must not be understood as a field of "phenomenological facts" since there is no such facts! Our so-called phenomenological experience is not some "pure" or "direct" experience of the world, but a conditioned and constructed perspective on experience. Again, this is why in chapter two I state that I am not a phenomenologist. The world-view I am developing demands an altogether different sensibility; a different perspective and way of thought. This complicates matters considerably, for I am attempting to unfold a different view of reality while forced to employ traditional tools and concepts. Nevertheless, despite such constraints, it is possible at least to approximate a description of situated realism, suggesting the possibility of experiencing in a counter-commonsensical mode.

In chapter two, I began to outline situated realism as a field of becoming; a field in constant flux that may be described as a surface of forces. All that we may call reality is already a relation of forces—a certain configuration of forces—constituting a body. And as Deleuze comments, such a body may be "chemical, biological, social or political" (1983, p. 40). What constitutes a body then is a certain configuration of forces. But describing reality in terms of a dynamic field of forces may suggest that forces are somehow what is "real" *behind* what is experienced, thereby reintroducing some Kantian thing in itself. However, this is not the case. Forces do not describe the "real" behind the "apparent," but are a certain mode, a certain way of describing experience. They are a means to articulate a world-view lived in some way. In addition, as indicated in chapter two, forces do not describe reality merely in a quantitative way but also qualitatively, introducing interpretation and valuation as key components of situated realism.

If what constitutes a body, then, is a certain configuration of forces with both a quantitative and a qualitative aspect, the question arises as to what guides any such configuration. For Nietzsche, the answer lies with will-to-power: "The victorious concept of 'force,' by means of which our physicists have created God and the world, still needs to be completed: an inner will must be ascribed to it, which I designate as 'will to power'" (1967, 619). But will-to-power is a problematic notion, especially when posited as an "ontological" principle. The reference to "will" introduces an anthropocentric element which is unnecessary for situated realism at least, adding an unwelcomed complication. Rejecting will-to-power as the guiding principle for the configuration of forces, however, does not entail a rejection of "power." Nietzsche was right to recognize the importance of power and its role in the configuration of chemical, biological, social or political bodies. And, as I indicate in chapter three, it is Foucault who attempted an analysis of the manifestation of power in various spheres.

What guides the relation of forces and allows for the formation of certain configurations and not others is power, understood in the constitutive sense I outline in chapter three. Put differently, the relations of forces constituting any particular body need to be recognized as power relations, for power is the relationship of force with another. It is not the case that "behind" forces there is some guiding principle or foundation called power, but the relation between forces is itself a power relation. Power, as the configuration of certain forces and not others, is immanent within experience, constituting a variety of diverse bodies. It manifests itself by seeking the formation of certain spaces with certain bodies while excluding others. In this way, it is, as Foucault remarks, "intentional and nonsubjective" (1978, p. 94). It is intentional because it is always directed at attaining a certain space, a certain configuration, so as to manifest itself. It is nonsubjective because as I indicated in chapter two, power is what constitutes any "subject" as a certain body; a certain configuration of forces.

Posited in this way, however, power appears as some unitary notion describing a monistic field, relegating difference and multiplicity to a secondary level. It appears with the notion of power, characterized as the relationship of forces, I am suggesting some overall unitary notion to characterize situated realism. This is not the case. To understand power immanently within the field of experience is to understand it *both* as a unitary notion and as a multiplicity and plurality. This, I believe, is similar to Nietzsche's conception of will-to-power. While for Nietzsche will-to-power suggested a unitary notion as indicated by such remarks as "a world whose essence is will to power" (1886/1966: 186), he posited it also as a multiplicity and a plurality. As Deleuze remarks, "[t]he monism of the will to power is inseparable from a pluralist typology" (1983, p. 86). When we speak of *the* will-to-power as a unitary notion, what is meant is the unity of a multiplicity, of a plurality of forces. At once, will-to-power is neither a unity nor a multiplicity but it is both. Similarly, power as I characterize it should not be understood as only a unitary notion. Power is unitary in the sense of configuring a certain relation of forces, but it is also a multiplicity and a plurality of forces configured. In this sense, power is a multiplicity and a plurality, everywhere all the time and yet nowhere at any one time when considered as unitary. Such a view of power, however, must not be considered as a view from nowhere, for as I will indicate shortly it describes a *situated* realism. As a field of flux, of becoming, the field of experience is a constant formation and destruction of differing constellations of forces. Power relations are constructed, manipulated, changed, and destroyed in a field in flux. As such, the unitary aspect of any configuration is simultaneous with the multiple and pluralist aspect of the field, rendering unity and difference as "two sides of the same coin," so to speak.

While simultaneous monism and pluralism may seem perplexing, it is, I believe, at the very heart of the world-view I am unfolding. It suggests an understanding of power not as some permanently fixed relationship between bodies, but as an unstable and loose association among multiple forces that may at any point strengthen or disintegrate. In this sense, the world-view I am advocating is that of a world in struggle where no particular body—be it social, political, chemical, or biological—can maintain itself indefinitely, once constructed, without a continuous manifestation of its power. And, as I will indicate shortly, this struggle is between interpretations and valuations.

If power, then, is relations of forces constituting a body, to "know" a body amounts to uncovering those forces, those power relations. But such "uncovering" must not be understood as "discovering" those "true" forces constituting any particular body. There are no such forces, for it is always a matter of a certain configuration of forces attempting to "uncover" another such configuration. Recall from the previous chapter, "subject" and "object," although individuated, both remain as relations of forces constructed through an immanent synthesis. This synthesis is none other than that of power relations. Consequently, to "know" any particular body is to have some configuration act upon another, synthesizing and constructing another configuration. What allows for such a process is the quality of forces manifested as interpretations and valuations.

As I have indicated, forces are not merely quantitative, but also qualitative. The quality of forces manifests itself as interpretation thus rendering any configuration of forces a complex of both a quantity and a quality of force. But the quality of forces manifested as interpretations does not provide a unique interpretation that is somehow the "true" interpretation of any particular body. Any body is a multiplicity, a plurality of forces with both a certain quantity and a quality. In their multiplicity, any such configuration of forces thus provides a plurality of senses to a body. There is no fixed essence to a body, no fixed identity remaining unchanged, but only a plurality of forces, of senses that are the result of different formations within the constellation of forces constituting a body. A body, then, may also be characterized as a constellation of senses, of different senses that define a phenomenon. And a phenomenon may have as many different senses as the forces that define it. As Deleuze writes: "The same object, the same phenomenon, changes sense depending on the force which appropriates it . . . . Sense is therefore a complex notion; there is always a plurality of senses, a constellation" (1983, p. 3).

To "know" a phenomenon, to "know" a body, amounts to interpreting it. It is a process where a particular constellation of forces interprets another. Put differently, it is a process whereby a particular power configuration interprets another such configuration. But since a body is a plurality of senses, interpreting a body amounts to a recognition that certain senses and not others constitute it. This implies that at the heart of interpretation is a process of valuation where certain senses are recognized over others. And as Deleuze correctly indicated (1983, pp. 3–8), valuation cannot be understood without the notion of hierarchy, for value is hierarchy. Given that a body is a plurality of senses, to interpret a body in any particular sense is to value certain senses over others such that what is higher in the hierarchy is recognized as the interpretation of a particular body.

There is no sense to any particular body without value, and given that a phenomenon is a complex, it manifests a plurality of senses and possibilities of different valuations. Thus interpretation is far from being a simple activity. It involves a certain dynamic within a field in flux characterized by power relations which are "known" through interpretation and valuation as a certain sense attributed to a body. Interpretation then, is the formation of a particular perspective, which is itself a complex, and the nature of any phenomenon depends upon the perspective formed. Since there is always a plurality of senses to any phenomenon, and possibilities of different valuations, there are numerous perspectives to any phenomenon depending upon the interpretation. This is not to suggest that some essence of the phenomenon is interpreted, but that interpretation constitutes a phenomenon with a particular sense and valuation. What a phenomenon is depends upon the interpretation and the forces taking hold of the phenomenon at the time. But since forces are in flux, there is never a moment that captures the being of the phenomenon. Any particular interpretation is already a particular perspective. This is what I believe Nietzsche meant when claiming: "'Essence,' the 'essential nature,' is something perspective and already presupposes a multiplicity" (1967, 556). It is always a question of interpretation, of arriving at a particular perspective, at a particular sense and valuation. A perspective, therefore, is the result of a double activity: of a particular sense and a particular valuation, resulting from an interpretation. This is why there can be no fixed identity, no constant essential nature. What a phenomenon is, what a body is, depends upon the interpretation. Crucially, however, the reference to "is" must not be understood in the traditional sense of some permanent and fixed being. If we must speak of being, then a phenomenon's being must be understood as a being in flux.

A question that may arise at this stage is "who then interprets and evaluates?" If by "who" we are to understand subjectivity as I indicate in chapter two, then it amounts to other constellations of forces, other power configurations, other bodies, and other perspectives that interpret. What or who interprets is another power configuration, another set of perspectives that is itself situated within a set of certain senses and values. If, for example, I were to consider myself as an interpreter, then, as a particular configuration of forces I interpret other bodies, other configurations so that I may "know" them. That is, I form perspectives, which amounts to establishing other senses and valuations of differing bodies. Thus, perspectives cannot be escaped. It is always a matter of forming perspectives on other perspectives through perspectives.

Perspectives, that is constellations of power relations, are what interpret. They seek to discover the sense and value of any phenomenon. That is why interpretation and evaluation are far from being simple activities. They require a careful unfolding of the forces constituting any phenomenon. But the issues involved are even more complex, for perspectives are not essences in any traditional sense, and are susceptible to change depending upon the variation in forces. Since forces describe a field in flux and are related within this field, any variation in the power configuration that interprets or is being interpreted, or in both, will generate a different perspective—a different sense and value.

This shifting nature of perspectives; this variation in senses and values, explains why, in chapter two, subjectivity is posited as a certain singularity with neither a fixed essence nor a stable identity. As a constellation of forces, subjectivity is itself constituted through perspectives. In this sense, perspectives are pre-subjective, constituting any sense of individuation. And since perspectives vary in sense and value, subjectivity can be understood only as a loosely defined notion signifying various senses and values. To borrow from Deleuze (1993, p. 20), we must not regard subjectivity as that from which variations in senses and values emanate, but as the condition in which such variations manifest themselves. To claim that a subject interprets or has a perspective on some subject is to claim that a perspective or set of perspectives interprets another set of perspectives. It is an interpretation of an interpretation, and not a description of what is not already an interpretation. As Foucault remarks:

> Interpretation can never be brought to an end, simply because there is nothing to interpret. There is nothing absolutely primary to interpret, because at bottom everything is already interpretation. Each sign is in itself not the thing that presents itself to interpretation, but the interpretation of other signs. (1990, p. 64)

The idea that perspectives, interpretations, and valuations are "primary" in the sense that they constitute what may be a "subject" or "object" may seem perplexing. This is especially so given the skeletal sketch of situated realism I have presented. The idea goes against our commonsense understanding of these terms which suggests that some subject must have a perspective or form interpretations and valuations, rather than be constituted by them. But this counter-intuitive aspect, I believe, is an integral part of situated realism since it is a world-view that demands an altogether different way of thinking and experiencing from what commonsense may suggest. Although I do not claim, nor do I believe, that situated realism characterizes Nietzsche's or Deleuze's philosophies, its close proximity to their views is evident in the manner I characterize situated realism. And in the spirit of their philosophies, I believe that a different way of thinking, of experiencing, and of living, demands some ability for experiencing senses that are not altogether commonsensical. Indeed, the originality and specificity of Nietzsche's philosophy is precisely its indicating to us the possibility of moving beyond common sense into realms previously not thought possible.

As a different way of thinking and of experiencing, situated realism directs us towards the possibility of remaining faithful to the field of experience in all of its richness. As with Nietzsche's and Deleuze's philosophies, it rests on an empiricism that does not seek to give an account of how the sensible becomes intelligible. It does not describe how a subject can experience the sensible, nor does it describe the necessary conditions for such a subject to have such an experience. It is not an empiricism that begins with a distinction between a subject and the field of experience, asking how such experience is possible. It is an empiricism that begins with "the concrete richness of the sensible" (Deleuze and Parnet, 1987, p. 54) and remains faithful to this field.

The perspectives and interpretations occupying the field of experience, occupy it without attempting to abstract generalizations from it which are in turn applied to the field. They are situated and remain specific to a particular interpretation without establishing any such interpretation as some fixed essence continuing through the field of becoming. The interplay of forces and power relations, which characterizes perspectives, is never brought to a resting point, and is, as such, never abstracted from the field of experience. What allows for such an empiricism is the distinction I make in chapter four between the negative conception of difference and real difference. Under situated realism it is real difference that is captured through perspectives and interpretations, which are the differences in the fluctuations of power and forces. Unlike Kant whose framework imposes an a priori structure on the sensible, situated realism captures the sensible within its field without imposing any a priori structures. It is not a question of a subject determining a given manifold, but of realizing some sense of subjectivity within a given manifold. The manifold is not adapted to the subject, but the subject is adapted to the manifold since the manifold constitutes the subject.

Power, forces, interpretations, valuations, and perspectives must not be understood as some ultimate constituents, or some ultimate principles determining the field of experience. Crucially, situated realism, like Nietzsche's empiricism, must not be understood as a return to some pre-Kantian notion of the empirical, but a return to the empirical that does not subjugate the field to knowledge, as does the Kantian synthesis. Power, forces, interpretations, valuations, and perspectives must be understood as tools for communicating through the real difference of the empirical without subjugating it. They are tools making it possible to experience this field as a field of real difference. They are not some absolute a priori structures imposed by a synthesizing subject, but tools which provide access to the field of experience, determining it while they are determined. While not being an essence of the sensible, for there is no such essence, these tools are at once the sensible—in that they constitute it—and an interpretation.

But if situated realism is characterized by power, forces, interpretations, valuations, and perspectives as tools constituting the field of experience, in what sense is this a "realist" world-view, and why is it situated? Also, how may it apply to psychotherapeutic practice? Focusing on the realist aspect first, I indicated earlier that a realist position need not appeal to an "independent reality" which we can directly access, whether in whole or part. A world-view may still count as realist if it recognizes reality as a certain force that restricts and constrains us in certain ways and not others; restricting the production of knowledge in such a way that it cannot be based on mere whim where "everything goes". If situated realism, then, is to be a realist position denying the epistemological-metaphysical thesis that appeals to a discoverable "independent reality," it must be a position that recognizes the restrictions imposed by "reality." The question then is: Are just any interpretations and perspectives possible within situated realism?

The answer to the question, of course, must come from within situated realism since it is the world-view under consideration. In other words, the question posed must be asking whether I, as a particular configuration of forces, can construct any or every perspective or interpretation depending only on my whims and desires. If the question does not come from within situated realism and is posed from an altogether different metaphysical position or world-view—with its particular understanding of subjectivity, perspectivism, and interpretation—it becomes irrelevant to situated realism. As a question posed within the confines of situated realism, the answer is a most emphatic no, for perspectives and interpretations are restricted in at least two crucial ways. First, as an interpreter I am a certain configuration of forces; of power relations that determine me in certain ways. In this sense, reality determines me and situates me in ways that are not of my own choosing. At this level, perspectives and interpretations are not manufactured by my whims and desires, but are what manufactures me! They constitute who I am as a certain individuated configuration ever changing in time. Second, as a configuration of forces that interprets, I am restricted by the power relations that constitute me and that which is being interpreted. It is these power relations, in both their quantitative and qualitative aspects, that determine what perspectives are constructed. In this sense, reality as a field of forces determines what configurations prevail. And what can be more realistic than that!

But there is a different sense in which the question "Are just any interpretations and perspectives possible within situated realism?" may be posed. It may be understood also as a question demanding an explanation for differentiating between what is "known" and what is mere phantasy, illusion, or personal belief or opinion. In other words, is it possible under situated realism to distinguish between "knowledge" and personal opinion or belief? Do some interpretations and perspectives constitute "knowledge" while others do not? The answer to these questions, once again, depends upon the restrictive role imposed by reality itself as a field of power relations. The kind or degree of resistance imposed by the field on any interpretation or perspective determines its nature. For example, I, as a particular body or configuration, may interpret another body in a certain way. The other body, as a certain configuration, manifests itself in a certain way. Its forces, as power relations with both a quantitative and a qualitative aspect, seek to manifest themselves in some specific manner. Whether my interpretation of the other body constitutes "knowledge" would depend on the kind or degree of resistance my power relations encounter with the other body. That is, my interpretation is tested within the field of experience itself. If I do not "know" the other body then its power relations would manifest themselves as counter to my expectations, thus presenting me with a resistance that would "awaken me" and require me to re-examine my belief, opinion, or phantasy. In other words, it is the field of experience itself that compels me to differentiate between what I do and do not "know."

In fact, the realism associated with situated realism may be considered "more real" than that associated with varieties of realism claiming direct access to an "independent reality." Such varieties, as I indicated earlier, define realism via a certain epistemological requirement—namely, that at least some aspect of an "independent reality" is directly knowable. But such an understanding of realism confines it to a certain epistemological thesis; to what can be "known." It subjugates realism to epistemology, thereby reintroducing a quasi-Kantian perspective that subjugates being to knowing. With situated realism, there is no such epistemological constraint, for the empirical realm, the field of experience, is primary and not dependent on what can or cannot be known. It demands an immersion within reality in all of its concrete richness. In this sense, situated realism is a much stronger affirmation of reality, recognizing its force in determining "subjects" and "objects."

But, as I have indicated, it is a *situated* realism also since the question of value and the hierarchy of values is at its very heart. To interpret is to evaluate, to form a perspective that establishes certain values over others. And if reality is characterized by interpretation and evaluation, then this world-view is a situated view, establishing the question of value as primary. Consequently, all questions and issues become debates on values; on which values are being promoted and which demoted. Whether we are in the realm of philosophy, politics, psychology, economics, or science, ultimately the debate is among competing values and power configurations seeking to manifest themselves. Of course, many would perhaps disagree with such a world-view, and would argue for another perspective. But arguing for a different world-view or perspective amounts to debating the promotion of competing values! With situated realism, the question of value is the world-view enabling it to be simultaneously a universal and situated world-view. This is an integral part of the values of situated realism. While claiming a universal outlook on the world, situated realism also recognizes its situated nature within itself. It posits itself as a characterization of the field of experience while allowing for the positing of other world-views. It posits itself as the center while simultaneously claiming that every point in the field is a center. To borrow from Debra Bergoffen, whose remarks are directed at Nietzsche's perspectivism, situated realism "is not grounded in the claim that this is the true perspective but in the affirmation that decentered perspectivism is less repressive than the absolute perspective of the center" (1990, p. 57).

Ultimately, however, part of the perplexing nature of situated realism stems from it being an experiential world-view. Consequently, language may be an extremely poor substitute for *experiencing* situated realism as a certain world-view. After all, "it is the stillest words which bring the storm. Thoughts that come on doves' feet guide the world" (Nietzsche, 1883–1885/1969: II, The Stillest Hour). And in being a philosophy of experience, it does not translate well into concrete examples without it becoming trivialized. This is why I have resisted presenting any such examples, for any example depends upon a whole series of interpretations and valuations.

Although it is beyond the scope of this study to articulate how situated realism translates to the clinical level, thus serving as a foundation for psychotherapeutic practice, it is useful to consider briefly what such an application implies. With respect to reconceptualizing both the client and the therapist, situated realism suggests an understanding of both as certain dynamic and fluid configurations of forces that remain always partial and incomplete, rather than static and determinate in specific ways. Consequently, the psychotherapeutic encounter becomes an interaction between two bodies, two relations of forces that may conflict, clash, harmonize, or repulse while simultaneously configuring and reconfiguring themselves. This view contrasts sharply with that of insight-oriented psychotherapy's, which suggests a perception of the client as some fixed entity awaiting "discovery" through the scientific treatment of an expert healer. Furthermore, contrary to the standard view of insight-oriented psychotherapy I presented in chapter one, which suggests the "discovery" of the client through the application of specific theories and methods, situated realism conceives as force relations both theories and methods. With respect to psychotherapeutic theories, situated realism indicates a conception of them as power structures rather than as windows onto reality. As power structures, they indicate an understanding of psychotherapeutic method as the forceful and transformative application of power rather than controlled, precise exploration.

 At a more concrete level, situated realism suggests an understanding of psychological "disorders," such as anxiety and depression that is based on perspectives, interpretations, and valuations and how they interact with other such configurations. Perhaps under situated realism, psychic "instability," "dysfunction," or "stress" are rooted in the degrees of resistance interpretations encounter within the field of experience. If such is the case, then situated realism suggests a reconceptualization of client problems and issues that prioritizes the question of value and interpretation. Such a move would entail the abandonment of universal characterizations of psychological "disorders," since psychological issues become specific to the particular configuration of forces. Consequently, "therapeutic improvement" or "cure" become the temporary reconfiguration of forces that constitute the client and her or his surrounding environment, such that the level of resistance encountered with other forces is reduced. This reduction in the level of resistance within the field of experience would allow the client to be more adaptive and more integrated. Again, such a view of "mental health" contrasts sharply with the belief that it is the achievement of some universal norm of well-being applicable to all persons with such and such problems.

 Finally, and perhaps most importantly, situated realism rejects understanding insight acquisition as the attainment of permanent, fixed "truths." As I indicated in chapter two, the reconceptualization of subjectivity as a fluid and dynamic configuration of forces indicates an understanding of insight and self-knowledge that is based upon re-evaluation and re-interpretation. In contrast, those who lack insight and self-knowledge live a life determined for them by their particular situation and the configuration of forces that constitutes them. However, insight acquisition under situated realism must not be understood as a static achievement, for re-evaluation and re-interpretation are constant activities that temporarily rearrange perspectives and shift power relations in a field that is in flux.

While the application of situated realism to clinical practice remains a project for future consideration, it is important to note that there has been some work done at the clinical level which suggests a conceptual framework similar to that of situated realism. Most notable in this regard is the work of the schizoanalyst Félix Guattari, whose views have had a profound impact on Deleuze and their collaborative efforts. In articulating his new or different form of analysis—schizoanalysis—Guattari develops a world-view that is similar to situated realism in which subjects are viewed as fluid and dynamic configurations of forces in relation with other configurations.

For Guattari, subjectivity, which is the focus of his work, is "manufactured" or "fabricated" through various forces and conditions that attempt "to mould the subjective positions of each individual" thereby producing a "serialized subjectivity" (Guattari, 1995, p. 194). Such a serialized subjectivity is manufactured through the application of categories such as age, race, and sex, which "pass through a long and complicated process involving the family, school, 'machinic' systems (like TV, various media, sports, etc.)" (p. 194). It is also manufactured through psychoanalysis and the various forms of psychotherapy that are yet another form of control. This manufacturing process results in a certain kind of a pseudo-unified subject whose desire and creativity are temporarily brought under control (p. 19). However, since "[t]he psyche, in essence, is the resultant of multiple and heterogeneous components" (p. 204), such fabricated subjectivity is bound to result in various psychological problems. In the language of situated realism, serialized subjects are much more likely to encounter a greater degree of resistance within the field of experience.

To counter such serialization, Guattari proposes schizoanalysis, which is posited as a replacement for psychoanalysis. Schizoanalysis is an attempt to free subjects from the constraints of a manufactured subjectivity, and thus allow for the unimpeded flow of desire.

> The work of the analyst, the revolutionary, and the artist meet to the extent that they must constantly tear down systems which reify desire, which submit the subject to the familial and social hierarchy. (I am a man, I am a woman, I am a son, I am a brother, etc.) No sooner does someone say, "I am this or that" than desire is strangled. (Guattari, 1995, p. 222)

This freeing of desire allows for the formation of "a different relation to the world" (p. 188), which entails a different subjectivity and a different relation with others. Moreover, it implies that schizoanalysis, unlike psychoanalysis, "is turned towards the future rather than fixated upon the stases of the past" (pp. 205–206). Its focus is to open new and different spaces for future creativity, rather than subsume desire under imprisoning familial and social categories. Crucially then, schizoanalysis must not be viewed as some alternative form of therapy with its own language and rituals, for that would simply entail the production of another serialized subject. For Guattari, schizoanalysis "is not an alternative modelization. It is the search for a meta-modelization. It attempts to understand how we got to this point" (1996, p. 275). Consequently, Guattari is not too specific about what is actually involved in the day-to-day clinical practice of schizoanalysis.

Guattari is not simply positing a new form of therapy that conforms to and reinforces existing social structures, but, like situated realism, he is unfolding a world-view with potentially revolutionary clinical and social implications. What is construed in terms of forces and power in situated realism, is rendered in terms of power and desire within Guattari's world-view. However, there remains a crucial difference between situated realism and Guattari's position. Under situated realism power is the relationship of forces where such forces have both a quantitative and a qualitative aspect. Through the qualitative dimension of forces we can understand the operation of desire and see how desire is an aspect of all configurations. For Guattari "[d]esire is power; power is desire" (1996, p. 20). That is, desire and power are identical for him which is not the case in situated realism. However, under both world-views desire is an immanent aspect of all configurations ("machines"), be they technological, chemical, biological, political, or economic (pp. 272–273). And this view of desire runs counter to the psychoanalytic view, which hopes

> to find raw desire, pure and hard, by heading off to look for knots, hidden in the unconscious, and secret keys of interpretation. Nothing can unravel, by the sheer magic of transfer, the real micropolitical conflicts that emprison the subject . . . . There is nothing to discover in the unconscious. The unconscious needs to be created. (Guattari, 1995, p. 180)

And, in psychoanalysis, it is created by "crushing desire" through psychoanalytic interpretations (p. 181). In other words, since "there is no universal structure of the human mind" (p. 220) psychoanalysis manufactures subjects through the "crushing" of their desires, which amounts to an absorption into familial categories.

What is required then at the clinical and social levels, is a "veritable molecular revolution" (p. 194). For Guattari, such a revolution involves the application of schizoanalysis to various psychological, technological, chemical, biological, political, or economic configurations so as to arrive at "a permanent reinvention" of subjectivity (p. 194). This is similar to the implications of situated realism and the revolution it suggests at the clinical and social levels. However, this application does not imply some uniform model applicable to all aspects of society or to all types of clients. Each configuration has to be reinvented or reconfigured in a unique way. At the clinical level, schizoanalysis, like situated realism, calls for a reconfiguration of subjectivity that allows it to be more creative and future oriented. As Guattari indicates, since "subjectivity . . . did not occur by itself, but was produced by certain conditions . . . these conditions could be modified through multiple procedures in a way that would channel it in a more creative direction" (p. 194).

My analysis in this chapter then, leads to two major conclusions. First, the "metaphysical" foundations of insight-oriented psychotherapies are extremely problematic, rendering as questionable the very foundations of such therapies. This entails that clients are not only absorbed into the therapist's philosophical framework during therapy, but they are absorbed into a problematic epistemological-metaphysical framework that relies on a questionable understanding of realism. Second, a rejection of the metaphysical foundations of insight-oriented psychotherapy does not entail a rejection of realism in favor of some antirealism. We can be realists and maintain a conception of knowledge as construction! As I have outlined with situated realism, a realist position is possible without an appeal to direct access to an "independent reality." And, as I have indicated, such a realist world-view may have psychotherapeutic application.

Six

ETHICAL CONSIDERATIONS

1. The Ethics of Insight-Oriented Psychotherapy

In a 1973 paper entitled "Psychotherapy as a Means of Social Control," Nathan Hurvitz argues that despite the many shortcomings of psychotherapy, particularly psychodynamic therapy, its social persistence is explained by its role as a means of social control. Through both its ideology and practice, which reinforce each other, "psychotherapy creates powerful support for the established order—it challenges, labels, manipulates, rejects, or co-opts those who attempt to change the society" (p. 237). In this way psychotherapy reinforces the "prevailing value system of the society" (p. 237) and serves as a means of social control.

Although Hurvitz's paper is now thirty-eight years old, much of what he argues is applicable to the contemporary practice of insight-oriented psychotherapy. As I have been indicating throughout the previous chapters, insight-oriented psychotherapy involves a practice whereby clients are drawn into the therapist's philosophical framework. This framework, characterized by a certain problematic conception of subjectivity, knowledge, and reality—which is a certain valuation of these notions—to a large extent reflects prevailing social attitudes. As a result, insight-oriented psychotherapy reinforces prevailing social values, at the philosophical level at least. Of course, one may question whether prevailing social attitudes in European and North American cultures at least, are reflected in the philosophical assumptions I have attributed to insight-oriented psychotherapists. Although I do not have any "concrete evidence" to support such a claim, my bet would be that the majority do uphold an epistemological-metaphysical framework similar to the one I attribute to insight-oriented psychotherapy. My claim here is simply that the majority of people do believe in some form of realism where reality is discoverable as it is in itself, and where objects in the world are directly accessible. This is usually coupled with a belief in the ontological reality of some "core" self or subject. And such beliefs may be true both within and outside the academy.

But we need not go as far as the philosophical underpinnings to indicate insight-oriented psychotherapists' adoption of prevailing social values, within their practice at least if not in their personal lives, and to show that these values are transferred to the client during therapy. Consider, for example, the question of suicide within European and North American cultures. For many, suicide or the desire to commit suicide is considered a problem. While it may be tolerated under certain circumstances, such as a severe illness, it is especially problematic when the underlying cause is psychological in nature. The idea that someone might commit suicide simply because it is the honorable thing to do is virtually non-existent within contemporary social values. If some individual does indicate honor, for example, as the reason to commit suicide, then almost always some other "mental problem" is read as the cause. Within the "mental health" profession, and among insight-oriented psychotherapies, similar views are upheld on the question of suicide. It would be difficult, if not impossible, to find a psychotherapist who would condone suicide on the grounds that it may be the honorable thing to do under certain psychological circumstances. Consider, for example, one of the Canadian Mental Health Association's pamphlets on suicide. Under "What Can You Do If You Are Feeling Suicidal?" it states, "[r]egaining your will to live is more important than anything else at the moment" (1993). But why should this be the case? Why is my will to live more important at the moment than my honor? It may well be that committing suicide is the virtuous thing to do!

Of course, there is a whole series of issues that may be raised with respect to suicide and honor, such as what constitutes honor in the first place. My point, however, is simply to indicate how, in many respects, psychotherapists do endorse social values which guide their practice. Indeed, with suicide, many jurisdictions legally require a psychotherapist to take some sort of preventative measure with a client who indicates such desires. And, as such, it is difficult to imagine a psychotherapist condoning suicide simply because it is the honorable thing to do. The more likely scenario is an attempt by the psychotherapist to "cure" the client in such a way that suicide is no longer an option. But what is such a "cure" if not an absorption into socially accepted values (Goffman, 1967, pp. 137–148)?

While my focus in this study has not been on specific values, but on the epistemological-metaphysical values clients are absorbed into—which underlie more specific values—the main point I wish to put across remains the same. Insight-oriented psychotherapies are involved in a process whereby clients are drawn into the therapist's epistemological-metaphysical framework, which is itself a reflection of a society's prevailing world-view. This process, which I do not believe is engaged in intentionally by any self-respecting psychotherapist, results in a form of social control, reinforcing accepted social values and relegating to the outside as "odd," "peculiar," "different," or even "ill," individuals whose values run counter to social norms. But, although such social practices do concern me in their attempt to erase counter-social values, this is not my principal ethical concern with insight-oriented psychotherapy. As Hurvitz indicates in his conclusion, "every society uses the means of control available to it" (1973, p. 237). This may include "the mass media, educational institutions, police, courts, etc., including theories and practicies [sic] of psychotherapy" (p. 237). Thus, to critique insight-oriented psychotherapy solely as a means of social control brings into question the larger issue of what it means to have a society with some prevailing set of values.

In fact, as I have claimed with situated realism, any body, be it social, political, chemical, or biological, is a certain configuration of forces, of power relations seeking to manifest themselves. And, of course, this applies to society as well as a certain body of forces. Thus, it is to be expected that it would attempt a manifestation of its values through various institutions, including the practice of psychotherapy. But this does not imply that forces within society cannot contest certain practices, raising concerns and attempting to reconfigure force relations. This ability to contest practices is why I indicate my concern with insight-oriented psychotherapy's social role, even though I may understand it.

My principal ethical concern with insight-oriented psychotherapy revolves around the deceptive aspect of the practice. What most concerns me from an ethical standpoint is not so much the (re)construction of subjectivity taking place during therapy, but the deceptive manner in which such (re)construction is performed. According to its self-presentation, insight-oriented psychotherapy is a practice whereby clients discover their "true" or "core" self, thus gaining insight into their "true" nature. As such, clients are led to believe that any so-called insight gained during the course of therapy is a discovery of their true self or nature. Coupled with such an understanding of themselves is a belief in the ontological reality of such a self and in the very possibility of discovering "facts" about it. In other words, their belief in the discovery of some "true" self is situated in the epistemological-metaphysical world-view characterizing such therapies, which implicitly assumes clients' adoption of this world-view. But, as I have been claiming throughout this study, if what is actually occurring is a process whereby clients are being absorbed and seduced into the therapist's philosophical framework, then insight-oriented psychotherapy is a deceptive practice; deceiving clients into adopting some pre-conceived social norms. Moreover, there is a secondary level of deception occurring, for not only is there no discovery taking place, but the epistemological-metaphysical framework clients are being seduced into is itself questionable. This double deception, I believe, raises some serious concerns since it runs counter to the avowal of "discovery" and "truth" made by insight-oriented psychotherapies.

Metaphorically speaking, consider the first section of *Thus Spoke Zarathustra* in which Friedrich Nietzsche speaks of the "three metamorphoses of the spirit: how the spirit shall become a camel, and the camel a lion, and the lion at last a child" (1883–1885/1969: Of the Three Metamorphoses). The first metamorphosis speaks of the development of the spirit from infancy to adulthood, where it is laden with all the values and knowledge given to it. It thus enters adulthood with a heavy, unquestioned burden. But soon, it discovers a need for freedom; a need to re-evaluate what it has been given. And so, the second metamorphosis occurs. The camel needs to become a lion, to question and bring into doubt all that has been given. Thus, the lion creates a space allowing for new creations and new values. But as a lion, the spirit cannot create. It must undergo its third metamorphosis and become a child; a new beginning that allows for the creation of new values.

With insight-oriented psychotherapy, however, the client remains stuck as a camel, unable to undergo the second metamorphosis and become a lion. Although the client is led to believe in insight-oriented psychotherapy as a means to undergo the second metamorphosis, this does not occur since the therapy is a mere re-configuration of the camel! A deceptive process takes place whereby the client unknowingly assumes another configuration of the camel while believing herself or himself to have undergone the second metamorphosis. And, what is more troubling, the re-configured camel is itself questionable.

I am, however, not suggesting that there is a deliberate effort by insight-oriented psychotherapists to deceive clients. On the contrary, I think most insight-oriented therapists do believe they are assisting clients in discovering themselves. But as a non-deliberate form of deception which presumably ranks lower in seriousness than any deliberate form, it nevertheless remains a form of deception and is thus of serious ethical concern. Of course, this particular valuation of insight-oriented psychotherapy is my valuation, and upholding a sense of situated realism, I cannot ground it in any moral or ethical principle. Ultimately, whether one considers a non-deliberate form of deception as a serious ethical concern, depends upon a question of values.

2. Objections and Replies

Given the world-view I have been advocating throughout this study—that is, situated realism—any ethical debate concerning what values are being adopted and what ought to be adopted, will depend to a large extent on the forces, power relations, interpretations, and perspectives manifested at that particular time. In this study, I have claimed that insight-oriented psychotherapy is a deceptive practice, suggesting a devaluation of its status as a socially acceptable enterprise. This claim, however, raises a series of possible objections, some of which I would like to consider now.

First, from a practical standpoint, one may object to my ethical critique by arguing that absorption does not really matter as long as it works and the client's condition improves. After all, one may argue, the whole purpose of psychotherapy is to treat those problems that drove the client to seek therapy in the first place. And if at the end of the process those conditions virtually disappear, enabling the client to live in a much less troubled way, what does it matter if absorption was involved in the process? Surely, one may add, helping a troubled client reintegrate into socially accepted norms is to be welcomed, even if the process involves absorption into the therapist's philosophical framework. In other words, what does it matter if a client is reconfigured in certain deceptive ways, if the end result is psychological improvement?

While the force of this objection is readily recognizable, its implications are troublesome. If the end result of insight-oriented psychotherapy is the primary focus irrespective of how such a result is arrived at, then the objection suggests that the end justifies the means. In other words, as long as the ends of insight-oriented psychotherapy—the alleviation of suffering, the reduction of pain—are considered "noble," it does not really matter if some unethical means are employed to achieve them. But is this acceptable? To begin with, what are the limits, if any, of the unethical means that may be employed, and who is to decide them? If improving the client's condition is the primary focus of therapy, then are any unethical means towards such an end acceptable, including physical harm? If not, what about some unethical means, then, which are not so unethical? For example, while physically harming a client might be clearly unacceptable as a means, reconfiguring and seducing a client into a socially acceptable world-view might not be so unethical. Similarly, while seducing clients into a framework is not as unethical as deceiving them, deception is not as unethical as physical harm.

This puzzle indicates the problematic nature of trying to decide on what are considered acceptable means. And to a large extent, of course, such limits will depend upon who is being asked. As far as I am concerned, both the reconfiguration of a client and their deception are unacceptable means, with the latter being more serious. Since I value difference and plurality over sameness and unity, the reconfiguration of a client and her or his absorption into what is ultimately the socially prevailing world-view, indicates to me a certain erasure of the client's real difference, which I find unacceptable. Of course, I may be asked why I find it unacceptable to erase the client's difference, which entails a questioning of the grounds underlying my values. But given situated realism, no such foundations are possible, for valuation is ultimately the art of interpretation, depending to a large extent on relations of forces. Although, as I indicated earlier, numerous social practices do attempt to control what is considered counter to their values, I believe such practices should be resisted and not reinforced within the psychotherapeutic setting, even at the cost of some psychic instability. With deception as a means, matters are more serious, not because deception per se is negative in some absolute sense, in all and every situation, but because within the psychotherapeutic setting it leaves clients with a false impression. Clients emerge from therapy believing that they have gained insight into their "true nature," and consequently employ this so-called newly discovered knowledge in the rest of their lives, while remaining ignorant of what actually transpired during the course of therapy. As such, the consequences of deception as a means reach much further than the ends it is supposed to serve. Clients continue to live the illusion of having discovered at least some "true" or "core" aspect of themselves well after the therapy has ended.

For some perhaps, such an illusion is acceptable, and consequently deception may rightfully be used as a means within insight-oriented psychotherapy. Personally, I do not find it acceptable and would much rather suffer the pains of psychic instability than lead a comfortable life full of illusions! But of course I am making these remarks as an outsider, being neither a client nor an insight-oriented psychotherapist. Being aware of what occurs within insight-oriented psychotherapy, I am deciding upon acceptable and unacceptable means. Typically, however, clients are not aware of the absorption and deception taking place. They do not knowingly choose these means to end their suffering. On the contrary, the means offered to them proclaim truth, insight, self-knowledge, and discovery. This framing raises the question: Would absorption and deception be ethically acceptable if clients were informed and freely choose such means?

Perhaps, if clients truly choose to be absorbed and deceived, the ethical concerns with insight-oriented psychotherapy would diminish. After all, it is quite conceivable that a suffering client would make such choices as long as the end result is a termination of, or at least a great reduction in, the suffering. Upon closer examination, however, the possibility of such a scenario is highly unlikely, for we are asking a client to knowingly accept the application of subtle mechanisms and to be knowingly deceived into accepting such absorption as genuine discovery. In short, for a client to choose such means in therapy, she or he must engage in an elaborate form of self-conscious self-deception! In order for clients to be truly informed, they must be fully aware of what is to take place. As such, consenting to the therapy implies an agreement to deceive one's self while being fully aware of this deception. It requires the client to claim: "I will pretend that I am discovering myself and gaining insight into my true nature even though I am fully aware this is not the case." This appears dubious, at the very least, and raises the issue of self-deception which is beyond the scope of this study. Suffice it to say, merely informing the client and obtaining her or his consent is not a simple matter. Moreover, it is not at all clear what insight-oriented psychotherapy itself would be, as a psychotherapeutic practice, if it explicitly acknowledged absorption, (re)construction, and deception. Would it still remain as a form of psychotherapy assisting in the "discovery" of, and attainment of insight into some "true" or "core" self? I am not sure that would be the case.

Finally, one may ask whether any form of psychotherapy is possible without absorption. That is, even if the deceptive factor is omitted, can any form of psychotherapy be practiced without clients being absorbed into the therapist's philosophical framework? This is a difficult question, for the mechanisms that entail absorption are extremely subtle and inevitably present in any psychotherapeutic encounter, if not any dialogical encounter. Indeed, as I indicated in chapter five, interpretation and power, which play a crucial role in absorption, are constitutive factors of reality, and consequently cannot be avoided. Nevertheless, I believe it remains possible to practice psychotherapy without absorbing clients into the therapist's philosophical framework. Although such a therapy is yet to be fully articulated, it would require psychotherapists to become much more aware of the philosophical issues associated with the foundation of their practice. Perhaps, in being better acquainted with epistemological and metaphysical issues, the tendency to impart onto the client any particular world-view could be avoided.

The ethical concerns then, with insight-oriented psychotherapy are quite substantial. Not only is it a practice inevitably leading to a form of social control, through reconfiguring clients and subtly seducing them into prevailing social values, it is also a deceptive practice. Through the promise of insight, self-knowledge, and self-discovery, it deceives clients into adopting a problematic world-view that serves only to reinforce its philosophical foundations. Unless one places a high degree of value on such practices, they are ethically questionable and ought to be re-evaluated.

CONCLUSION

In many ways this work is a study in ethics. Indeed, given the world-view I suggest in chapter five, the implication is that ultimately philosophy is ethics, where ethics is construed broadly as pertaining to the question of value. Although philosophical questions may be debated at various levels asking for the internal consistency of a particular position, for example, there is a point reached where the debate ends and the choices made depend upon values. By this, I do not mean we cannot debate issues or stances, nor do I mean we cannot advocate certain positions over others, but that ultimately what we are advancing or advocating are certain values, and a certain world-view. Typically, however, the response to what I am suggesting is that even if no value-free positions exist, that does not imply we should not aspire to such ideals.

Consider, once again, the question of value in science. According to Susan Haack:

> Even if it were true that scientists are never entirely without prejudice, even if it were impossible that they should entirely put their prejudices out of sight when judging the evidence for a theory, it doesn't follow that it is proper to allow prejudice to determine theory choice. (No doubt it is impossible to make science perfect; it doesn't follow that we shouldn't try to make it better.) (1993, p. 562)

But what does Haack's position mean if it is impossible to put prejudices aside, as I have been suggesting in the previous chapters? If it is impossible to put prejudices aside, then either you abandon science as an enterprise, or you admit that it is infused with scientists' values. In other words, if practice is what matters, what ought to be done is irrelevant here if it is impossible to put aside prejudices. If science is going to be practiced, and if the values of scientists are epistemically significant, then it is a question of debating values. Alternatively, Haack may be suggesting that less prejudice is better than more prejudice, and that just because it is impossible to avoid prejudice, it does not follow that we should not aim for less of it in science. But if this is Haack's argument, then she misses the point entirely, which is that there is no value-free position from which to practice science. And if that is the case, the question of more or less value is irrelevant. Perhaps we may be able to debate which values to include and which to exclude, assuming we are aware of *all* the values in any particular situation, but to debate more or less values in a practice that cannot be value-free is of little practical consequence. Put differently, such a debate would, in practice, be about which values to substitute for some other set of values. Indeed, the demand for less values and the ideal of a value-free science are value claims themselves!

As I have attempted to indicate with situated realism, the question of values permeates thought, and if we ask the question "why?" often enough we arrive at the axiological dimension of any supposedly value-free position. The fact/value distinction implicit in Haack's remarks on more and less values, is irrelevant if *practice* is our main concern. And given my understanding of philosophy as practice, which I indicate in the introduction, philosophical reflection then, itself eventually reaches a point where it is a reflection on values. If this is so, what can be concluded from this study?

At the more general level, it would be accurate to conclude that, at the very least, this study advocates a re-evaluation of values manifested in the psychotherapeutic practices of insight-oriented psychotherapies. These values include those manifested through the alleged claims of such practices—claims to insight, self-discovery, and self-knowledge—as well as those exhibited through absorption, construction, and the world-view assumed by such therapies. It would be accurate to conclude also that such a re-evaluation occurs in the preceding chapters, from which certain conclusions may be drawn.

First, although it may seem as though I am advocating against the use of insight-oriented psychotherapies, I am not. I believe that until a viable alternative is found, insight-oriented psychotherapies are a "necessary evil" required for the "treatment" of some, where the "damage" done through such therapies is less than the alternative of no therapy at all. However, this does not imply that certain aspects of such practices cannot be changed or altered. For example, the deceptive dimension may be reduced or minimized, not through informing clients as I consider in chapter six, but by psychotherapists refraining from the use of language that suggests the discovery of some "true" or "real" self. Of course, this does not imply eradicating the deceptive factor, but it may minimize it.

Second, although the factors I indicate in chapter three are intrinsic to the psychotherapeutic encounter, the absorption they entail may be reduced if psychotherapists become more aware of these factors and the role they play. As I suggest in chapter six, a better understanding of the role of power, interpretation, suggestion, the form of the question, and other factors may reduce the potential for absorption. Crucially, however, such increased understanding must come with a much greater awareness of the epistemological and metaphysical issues associated with insight-oriented therapies. Perhaps then, if insight-oriented psychotherapists are to take a greater interest in the philosophical foundations of their practice and in the philosophical issues surrounding their practice, absorption may be reduced.

Third, as I indicate at the end of chapter five, the alternative worldview I present may suggest an alternative foundation for psychotherapy. However, I do not present it as a blueprint for an alternative form of psychotherapy, but as an alternative world-view to the one assumed by insight-oriented psychotherapies. Situated realism, however, does indicate a direction for an alternative form of therapy that does not succumb to the critique of insight-oriented psychotherapy I have presented. Briefly, this critique maintains that fundamentally, the problematic nature of insight-oriented psychotherapy rests upon the questionable world-view it assumes and imparts to the client. Thus, confronting any alternative form of therapy we need to ask two basic questions. First, does it assume a problematic world-view? And second, are clients being absorbed into this world-view? The answer to the first question may conceivably be "no." There is nothing in principle that prevents the formulation of a non-problematic world-view. However, with the second question, matters are not so simple. Given the intrinsic role of factors such as suggestion, power, and interpretation in any therapeutic encounter, the possibility of imparting a specific world-view to the client remains high. In other words, any therapy that assumes a certain world-view—a certain epistemological-metaphysical-ethical understanding—is at risk of being a type of therapy wherein clients adopt the therapist's world-view. This requirement entails one of two choices: either the therapy does not assume any world-view, which is impossible, or it assumes a whole multiplicity of world-views. In other words, if the therapeutic practice is not founded upon any particular epistemological-metaphysical-ethical assumptions then the client cannot be absorbed into any particular world-view. That is, the client cannot be absorbed into any particular understanding of subjectivity, knowledge, and reality.

I do not know whether it is possible to devise a therapeutic practice that assumes a multiple philosophical foundation; one that assumes, for example, an epistemological stance where knowledge is both discovered and constructed! But I do believe situated realism indicates the faint possibility of such a practice in being a stance that characterizes a world-view, which recognizes its situated nature within itself, while simultaneously positing a universal outlook. Such a world-view, coupled with its experiential dimension that I indicate in chapter five, may suggest a direction for a therapeutic practice with multiple philosophical foundations. However, it may be argued that the multiple philosophical foundations of any therapeutic practice themselves constitute a particular world-view, which the client may be absorbed into. While this risk is a theoretical possibility, I do not believe it is possible in practice, for although a therapist may assume a whole multiplicity of philosophical stances during the course of therapy, such an assumed multiplicity is not viable for everyday living. That is, even if a therapeutic practice upholding a variety of epistemological, metaphysical, and ethical views is possible, that does not imply it is possible to live everyday life assuming such a philosophical foundation.

Finally, even if no specific conclusions can be drawn from this study, and even if the reader contests the claims I have made, I hope that by asking the questions and reflecting on the answers, I have contributed in some minimal way to rupturing those mechanisms through which subjects are made. That we, as a "civil" society, will continue to manufacture subjects seems inevitable. I can only hope that at least a few may be constructed differently.

WORKS CITED

Babich, B. E. 1994. *Nietzsche's Philosophy of Science*. New York: State University of New York Press.

Basch, M. 1980. *Doing Psychotherapy*. New York: Basic Books.

Bergoffen, D. B. 1990. Nietzsche's Madman: Perspectivism without Nihilism. In *Nietzsche as Postmodernist,* ed. C. Koelb. New York: State University of New York Press.

Blanck, G. and R. Blanck. 1994. *Ego Psychology: Theory and Practice*. 2nd. ed. New York: Columbia University Press.

Brook, A. 1994. *Kant and the Mind*. New York: Cambridge University Press.

Calestro, K. M. 1972. Psychotherapy, Faith Healing, and Suggestion. *International Journal of Psychiatry* 10: 83–113.

Canadian Mental Health Association. 1993. Preventing Suicide. Toronto, Canada.

Code, L. 1981. Is the Sex of the Knower Epistemologically Significant? *Metaphilosophy* 12: 267–76.

———. 1991. *What Can She Know? Feminist Theory and the Construction of Knowledge*. Ithaca, New York: Cornell University Press.

———. 1995. *Rhetorical Spaces: Essays on Gendered Locations*. New York: Routledge.

Deleuze, G. 1983. *Nietzsche and Philosophy*, trans. H. Tomlinson. London: Athlone Press.

———. 1988. *Foucault*, trans. and ed. S. Hand. Minneapolis: University of Minnesota Press.

———. 1989. *Cinema 2: The Time-Image*, trans. H. Tomlinson and R. Galeta. Minneapolis: University of Minnesota Press.

———. 1990. *The Logic of Sense*, trans. M. Lester with C. Stivale. London: Athlone Press.

———. 1993. *The Fold: Leibniz and the Baroque*, trans. T. Conley. Minneapolis: University of Minnesota Press.

——— and F. Guattari. 1983. *Anti-Oedipus*, trans. R. Hurley, M. Seem, and H. R. Lane. Minneapolis: University of Minnesota Press.

——— and F. Guattari. 1987. *A Thousand Plateaus*, trans. B. Massumi. Minneapolis: University of Minnesota Press.

——— and C. Parnet. 1987. *Dialogues*, trans. H. Tomlinson and B. Habberjam. London: Athlone Press.

_____ and F. Guattari. 1994. *What is Philosophy?* trans. H. Tomlinson and G. Burchell. New York: Columbia University Press.

Dreyfus, H. L. and P. Rabinow. 1983. *Michel Foucault: Beyond Structuralism and Hermeneutics.* 2nd ed. Chicago: University of Chicago Press.

Ehrenwald, J. 1966. *Psychotherapy: Myth and Method.* New York: Grune & Stratton.

Emerson, Ralph Waldo. (1841/1903–1904) *The Complete Works of Ralph Waldo Emerson: Essays First Series*, Volume 2. Boston and New York: Houghton, Mifflin, and Company.

Erwin, E. 1997. *Philosophy and Psychotherapy: Razing the Troubles of the Brain.* California: Sage publications.

Farrell, B. A. 1981. *The Standing of Psychoanalysis.* Oxford: Oxford University Press.

Festinger, L. 1957. *A Theory of Cognitive Dissonance.* Stanford, CA: Stanford University Press.

Feyerabend, P. 1975. *Against Method: Outline of an Anarchistic Theory of Knowledge.* London: New Left Books.

Fiumara, G. C. 2002. The Development of Hermeneutic Prospects. In *Feminist Interpretations of Hans-Georg Gadamer*, ed. L. Code. University Park, Pennsylvania: Pennsylvania State University Press.

Foucault, Michel. 1970. *The Order of Things.* New York: Vintage.

_____. 1978. *The History of Sexuality. Volume I: An Introduction*, trans. R. Hurley. New York: Vintage Books.

_____. 1983. Why Study Power: The Question of the Subject. In Dreyfus and Rabinow, *Michel Foucault: Beyond Structuralism and Hermeneutics*. Written in English by Michel Foucault.

_____. 1990. Nietzsche, Freud, Marx, trans. A. D. Schrift. In *Transforming the Hermeneutic Context: From Nietzsche to Nancy*, ed. G. L. Ormiston and A.D. Schrift. Albany: State University of New York Press.

Fox, K. J. 2001. Self-Change and Resistance in Prison. In *Institutional Selves: Troubled Identities in a Postmodern World*, ed. J. F. Gubrium and J. A. Holstein. New York: Oxford University Press.

Frank, J. D. 1987. Psychotherapy, Rhetoric, and Hermeneutics: Implications for Practice and Research. *Psychotherapy* 24 (3): 293–302.

_____. 1989. Non-specific aspects of treatment: The view of a psychotherapist. In *Non-Specific Aspects of Treatment*, ed. M. Shepherd and N. Sartorius. Toronto: H. Huber.

Freud, S. 1909/1953–74. *The Standard Edition of the Complete Psychological Works of Sigmund Freud.* 24 Vols. Translated under the general editorship of J. Strachey. London: Hogarth Press.

_____. 1915/1953–1974. *The Standard Edition of the Complete Psychological Works of Sigmund Freud.* 24 Vols. Translated under the general editorship of J. Strachey. London: Hogarth Press.

_____. 1917/1953–1974. *The Standard Edition of the Complete Psychological Works of Sigmund Freud.* 24 Vols. Translated under the general editorship of J. Strachey. London: Hogarth Press.

_____. 1937/1953–74. *The Standard Edition of the Complete Psychological Works of Sigmund Freud.* 24 Vols. Translated under the general editorship of J. Strachey. London: Hogarth Press.

Frosch, J. 1990. *Psychodynamic Psychiatry: Theory and Practice.* Madison, Conn.: International Universities Press.

Gabbard, G. O. 1994. *Psychodynamic Psychiatry in Clinical Practice: The DSM-IV Edition.* Washington, DC.: American Psychiatric Press.

Gadamer, H. 1975/1989. *Truth and Method.* 2nd rev. ed. Tran. J. Weinsheimer and Donald G. Marshall. New York: Crossroad Publishing.

Gaylin, W. 2000. *Talk is Not Enough: How Psychotherapy Really Works.* Boston: Little Brown.

Glaser, S. 1980. Rhetoric and Psychotherapy. In *Psychotherapy Process: Current Issues and Future Directions*, ed. M. Mahoney. New York: Plenum Press.

Goffman, E. 1967. *Interaction Ritual: Essays on Face-to-Face Behavior.* New York: Pantheon Books.

Greenberg, J. R. and S. A. Mitchell. 1983. *Object Relations in Psychoanalytic Theory.* Cambridge, Massachusetts: Harvard University Press.

Grimm, R. H. 1979. Circularity and Self-Reference in Nietzsche. *Metaphilosophy* 10: 289–305.

Grünbaum, A. 1984. *The Foundations of Psychoanalysis: A Philosophical Critique.* California: University of California Press.

_____. 1993. *Validation in the Clinical Theory of Psychoanalysis: a Study in the Philosophy of Psychoanalysis.* Madison, CT: International Universities Press, Inc.

Guattari, F. 1995. *Chaosophy*, ed. S. Lotringer. New York: Semiotext[e].

_____. 1996. *Soft Subversions*, ed. S. Lotringer, trans. D. L. Sweet and C. Wiener. New York: Semiotext[e].

Gutting, G. 1989. *Michel Foucault's Archaeology of Scientific Reason.* New York: Cambridge University Press.

Haack, S. 1993. Knowledge and Propaganda: Reflections of an Old Feminist. *Partisan Review* Fall: 556–564.

Hacking, I. 1995. *Rewriting the Soul: Multiple Personality and the Sciences of Memory*. New Jersey: Princeton University Press.

Haraway, D. 1991. Situated Knowledges: The Science Question in Feminism and the Privilege of Partial Perspective. In *Simians, Cyborgs, and Women: The Reinvention of Nature*. London: Free Association Books.

_____. 1997. *Modest_Witness@Second_Millennium*. New York: Routledge.

Heidegger, M. 1927/1962. *Being and Time*, trans. J. Macquarrie and E. Robinson. New York: Harper & Row.

_____. 1937–40/1987. *Nietzsche. Volume III: The Will to Power as Knowledge and as Metaphysics*, trans. J. Stambaugh, D. F. Krell and F. A. Capuzzi. New York: Harper & Row.

_____. 1940–6/1982. *Nietzsche. Volume IV: Nihilism*, trans. F. A. Capuzzi. New York: Harper & Row.

Held, B. 1995. *Back to Reality: A Critique of Postmodern Theory in Psychotherapy*. New York: W.W. Norton.

Hume, D. 1739–1740/1978. *A Treatise of Human Nature*. 2nd edition, ed. L.A. Selby-Bigge. Oxford: Oxford University Press.

Hurvitz, N. 1973. Psychotherapy as a Means of Social Control. *Journal of Consulting and Clinical Psychology*. 40 (2): 232–239.

Jacobs, M. 1999. *Psychodynamic Counselling in Action*. 2nd ed. London: Sage.

Jopling, D. 1998. "First Do No Harm": Over-Philosophizing and Pseudo-Philosophizing in Philosophical Counselling. *Inquiry: Critical Thinking Across the Disciplines* XVII (3): 100–112.

_____. 2000. *Self-knowledge and the Self*. New York: Routledge.

_____. 2001. Placebo Insight: The Rationality of Insight-Oriented Psychotherapy. *Journal of Clinical Psychology* 57: 19–36.

_____. 2008. *Talking Cures and Placebo Effects*. Oxford: Oxford University Press.

Kant, I. 1787/1933. *Critique of Pure Reason*, trans. Norman Kemp Smith as *Immanuel Kant's Critique of Pure Reason*. 2nd edition. London: Macmillan.

Keller, E. F. and H. E. Longino, eds. 1996. *Feminism and Science*. Oxford: Oxford University Press.

Kohut, H. 1971. *The Analysis of the Self*. New York: International Universities Press.

Works Cited

Kottler, J. A. and R.W. Brown. 2000. *Introduction to Therapeutic Counseling: Voices from the Field.* 4th edition. Belmont, CA: Brooks/Cole Thomson Learning.

Kuhn, T. S. 1970. *The Structure of Scientific Revolutions.* 2nd ed. Chicago: University of Chicago Press.

Laurence, M. 1964. *The Stone Angel.* Toronto: McClelland and Stewart.

Loseke, D. R. 2001. Lived Realities and Formula Stories of "Battered Women." In *Institutional Selves: Troubled Identities in a Postmodern World*, ed. J. F. Gubrium and J. A. Holstein. New York: Oxford University Press.

May, R. 1983. *The Discovery of Being: Writings in Existential Psychology.* New York: Norton.

McLeod, J. and J. McLeod. 1993. The relationship between personal philosophy and effectiveness in counsellors. *Counselling Psychology Quarterly* 6 (2): 121–129.

Messer, S. B. and C. Seth Warren. 1995. *Models of Brief Psychodynamic Therapy: A Comparitive Approach.* New York: Guildford Press.

Nietzsche, F. 1883-5/1969. *Thus Spoke Zarathustra*, trans. R. J. Hollingdale. New York: Penguin. References by part numbers and section title.

———. 1886/1966. *Beyond Good and Evil*, trans. W. Kaufmann. New York: Vintage. References by section number.

———. 1887/1967. *On the Genealogy of Morals*, trans. W. Kaufmann and R. J. Hollingdale. In *On the Genealogy of Morals and Ecce Homo.* New York: Vintage. Referenced by essay and section numbers.

———. 1967. *The Will to Power*, trans. W. Kaufmann and R. J. Hollingdale. New York: Vintage. References by section number.

Okruhlik, K. 1992. Birth of a New Physics or Death of Nature? In *Women and Reason*, ed. E. Harvey and K. Okruhlik. Ann Arbor: University of Michigan Press.

Olkowski, D. 1990. Monstrous Reflection: Sade and Masoch—Rewriting the History of Reason. In *Crisis in Continental Philosophy,* ed. A. B. Dallery and C. E. Scott with P. Holley Roberts. New York: State University of New York Press.

Overholser, J. C. 1993. Elements of the Socratic Method: I. Systematic Questioning. *Psychotherapy* 30 (1): 67–74.

Perls, F. 1973. *The Gestalt Approach and Eye Witness to Therapy.* Ben Lomond, CA: Science and Behavior Books.

Plato. 1952. Phaedrus. In *Plato's Phaedrus*, trans. R. Hackforth. New York: Cambridge University Press.

———. 1963. Republic. In *The Collected Dialogues of Plato*, ed. E. Hamilton and H. Cairns. New Jersey: Princeton University Press.

_____. *Sophist*. In *The Collected Dialogues of Plato*.

_____. *Philebus*. In *The Collected Dialogues of Plato*.

_____. *Parmenides*. In *The Collected Dialogues of Plato*.

Pols, E. 1992. *Radical Realism: Direct Knowing in Science and Philosophy*. Ithaca, New York: Cornell University Press.

_____. 1998. *Mind Regained*. Ithaca, New York: Cornell University Press.

Ricoeur, P. 1970. *Freud and Philosophy: An Essay in Interpretation*, trans. D. Savage. New Haven, Conn.: Yale University Press.

_____. 1977. The Question of Proof in Freud's Psychoanalytic Writings. *Journal of the American Psychoanalytic Association* 25: 835–71.

Rogers, C. R. 1951. *Client-Centered Therapy: Its Current Practice, Implications, and Theory*. Boston: Houghton Mifflin Company.

Rorty, R. 1986. Freud and Moral Reflection. In *Pragmatism's Freud: The Moral Disposition of Psychoanalysis*, ed. J. H. Smith and W. Kerrigan. Baltimore: Johns Hopkins Press.

Rosenthal, D. 1955. Changes in Some Moral Values Following Psychotherapy. *Journal of Clinical Psychology* 19 (6): 431–6.

Rouse, J. 1996. Feminism and the Social Construction of Scientific Knowledge. In *Feminism, Science, and the Philosophy of Science*, ed. L. H. Nelson and J. Nelson. Boston: Kluwer Academic Publishers.

Russon, J. 2003. *Human Experience: Philosophy, Neurosis, and the Elements of Everyday Life*. New York: SUNY Press.

Sartre, J. P. 1943/1956. *Being and Nothingness*, trans. H. E. Barnes. New York: Washington Square Press.

Schafer, R. 1976. *A New Language for Psychoanalysis*. New Haven: Yale University Press.

Schmideberg, M. 1939. The Role of Suggestion in Analytic Therapy. *Psychoanalytic Review* XXVI: 219–229.

Spence, D. 1982. *Narrative Truth and Historical Truth: Meaning and Interpretation in Psychoanalysis*. New York: W. W. Norton & Company.

Spinelli, E. 2005. *The Interpreted World: An Introduction to Phenomenological Psychology*. 2nd ed. London: Sage Publications.

Strupp, H. 1972. Needed: A Reformulation of the Psychotherapeutic Influence. *International Journal of Psychiatry* 10: 114–120.

_____. 1992. Humanism and Psychotherapy: A Personal Statement of the Therapist's Essential Values. In *The Restoration of Dialogue: Readings in the Philosophy of Clinical Psychology*, ed. R. B. Miller. Washington, DC: American Psychological Association.

_____ and J. L. Bender. 1984. *Psychotherapy in a New Key: A Guide to Time-Limited Dynamic Psychotherapy*. New York: Basic Books.

Szasz, T. 1978. *The Myth of Psychotherapy*. New York: Anchor Press.

van Deurzen, E.1998. *Paradox and Passion in Psychotherapy: An Existential Approach to Therapy and Counselling*. New York: John Wiley and Sons.

Waelder, R. 1962. Review of *Psychoanalysis, Scientific Method and Philosophy*, ed. S. Hook. *Journal of the American Psychoanalytic Association* 10: 617–637.

Watters, E. and R. Ofshe. 1999. *Therapy's Delusions*. New York: Scribner.

Wegrocki, H. 1934. The Effect of Prestige Suggestibility on Emotional Attitudes. *The Journal of Social Psychology* V: 384–94.

Wisdom, J. 1969. *Philosophy and Psycho-Analysis*. Berkeley: University of California Press.

Wittgenstein, L. 1958. *Philosophical Investigations*, trans. G. E. M. Anscombe. Oxford: Basil Blackwell.

Yalom, I. D. 1980. *Existential Psychotherapy*. New York: Basic Books.

_____.1989. *Love's Executioner and Other Tales of Psychotherapy*. New York: Basic Books.

Yontef, G. and L. Jacobs. 2000. Gestalt Therapy. In *Current Psychotherapies*, ed. R. J. Corsini and D. Wedding. 6th edition. Itasca, IL: F. E. Peacock.

ABOUT THE AUTHOR

Hakam H. Al-Shawi is an Iraqi-Canadian academic and diplomat. Educated in England and Canada, he received his Bachelor of Arts degree with distinction in Economics from Carleton University. After a brief stint at Cambridge University, he returned to Canada to pursue his passion—philosophy. After completing a Master of Arts degree in philosophy in 2004 he received his Ph.D. in philosophy from York University, Canada, specializing in the philosophy of psychology. His research interests focus on "philosophy as practice" with a particular emphasis on the application of philosophy to daily life. Employing both existentialist and poststructuralist tools in much of his writing, he continues his research on philosophy as an aid to creating a life. He has published various articles in academic journals and has taught philosophy at both York University, Toronto, Canada, and at Sheridan College, Ontario, Canada. He is a founding member of the Canadian Society for Philosophical Practice and remains a non-resident research fellow at Bayt Al-Hikma in Baghdad, Iraq. In 2007 he was appointed as a diplomat at the Foreign Service Institute of the Iraqi Ministry of Foreign Affairs and was subsequently posted to Montreal, Canada, serving as both Consul and Deputy Head of Mission.

INDEX

a priori, 27, 28, 32, 33, 82, 90, 105
absorption, 2, 3, 8, 17, 43, 48, 52, 55, 58, 59, 60, 63, 110, 114, 116, 117, 118, 122
antirealism, 4, 9, 81, 88, 89, 95, 111
anxiety, 5, 14, 68, 108
Babich, B. E., 71, 125
Basch, M., 18, 125
Bender, J. L., 6, 131
Bergoffen, D., 107, 125
Brook, Andrew, 11, 29, 125
Brown, R. W., 7, 127, 129
Buddhism, 40
Calestro, K. M., 10, 46, 50, 51, 125
Canadian Mental Health Association, 114, 125
client conformity, 45, 47
client-centered therapy, 5, 16
Code, Lorraine, 11, 71, 72, 73, 83, 84, 90, 125, 126
consciousness, 29, 30, 31, 36, 67
cure, 18, 19, 21, 108, 114
Da-sein, 79
Deleuze, Gilles, 1, 2, 32, 37, 39, 56, 70, 74, 77, 83, 90, 99, 100, 102, 103, 104, 109, 125
depression, 5, 108
Descartes, René, 25, 26, 31, 79
difference, 3, 29, 70, 75, 76, 77, 78, 79, 85, 100, 104, 105, 110, 117
Dreyfus, H. L., 57, 126
Ehrenwald, J., 46, 126
embodiment, 3, 80
empiricism, 77, 82, 104, 105
Erwin, Edward, 19, 24, 58, 126
essence, 16, 53, 74, 100, 101, 102, 103, 104, 105, 109
existential therapy, 13, 65
facticity, 65
Farrell, B., 19, 46, 126
fascism, 3, 42, 77
Festinger, L., 51, 126
Feyerabend, P., 71, 126
Fiumara, Gemma C., 54, 126
Fliess, Wilhelm, 19

forces, 11, 1, 3, 5, 15, 35, 37, 38, 39, 40, 41, 42, 47, 48, 55, 56, 57, 70, 71, 73, 76, 78, 79, 81, 83, 84, 90, 99, 100, 101, 102, 103, 104, 105, 106, 108, 109, 110, 115, 116, 117
forgetfulness, 35, 40
Foucault, Michel, 1, 32, 37, 56, 57, 77, 90, 100, 103, 125, 126, 127
Fox, K., 60, 126
Frank, Jerome, 10, 11, 12, 51, 52, 126
Freud, Sigmund, 6, 18, 19, 20, 21, 22, 34, 48, 49, 65, 67, 126, 127, 130
Frosch, J., 16, 127
Gabbard, G., 17, 127
Gadamer, Hans-Georg, 53, 54, 55, 126, 127
Gaylin, W., 16, 127
gestalt therapy, 5
Glaser, S., 52, 127
Goffman, E., 114, 127
Greenberg, J. R., 6, 127
Grimm, R., 98, 127
Grünbaum, Adolf, 19, 20, 21, 22, 51, 127
Guattari, Félix, 39, 77, 109, 110, 111, 125, 126, 127
Haack, Susan, 121, 122, 128
Hacking, Ian, 34, 128
Haraway, D., 71, 73, 78, 80, 81, 83, 88, 90, 128
Heidegger, Martin, 26, 78, 79, 80, 128
Held, Barbara, 22, 23, 33, 52, 75, 76, 88, 89, 90, 91, 92, 93, 94, 128
Hume, David, 31, 82, 83, 90, 128
Hurvitz, N., 113, 114, 128
Husserl, Edmund, 73
insight, 1, 2, 3, 4, 5, 6, 7, 8, 9, 10, 11, 12, 13, 14, 15, 16, 17, 18, 19, 20, 21, 22, 23, 24, 25, 26, 28, 30, 31, 33, 34, 35, 36, 39, 40, 41, 43, 45, 46, 47, 48, 49, 51, 52, 54, 55, 56, 57, 58, 59, 60, 63, 64, 65, 66, 67, 68, 69, 70, 71, 73, 75, 78, 84, 87, 88, 89, 90, 93, 94, 98, 108, 111,

113, 114, 115, 116, 117, 118, 119, 122
interpretation, 7, 19, 21, 22, 37, 40, 41, 42, 47, 53, 55, 58, 66, 76, 83, 99, 101, 102, 103, 104, 105, 106, 107, 108, 110, 117, 119, 122, 123
Jacobs, L., 6, 16, 128, 131
Jopling, David, 11, 6, 10, 11, 12, 13, 14, 46, 47, 50, 51, 52, 64, 128
Kant, Immanuel, 3, 25, 26, 27, 28, 29, 30, 31, 32, 33, 36, 43, 44, 76, 82, 83, 90, 97, 105, 125, 128
Keller, E. F., 71, 128
knowledge, 1, 2, 3, 7, 8, 9, 11, 12, 15, 24, 26, 27, 31, 32, 33, 34, 35, 36, 37, 39, 40, 41, 45, 46, 47, 50, 51, 54, 57, 60, 63, 65, 66, 67, 68, 69, 70, 71, 72, 73, 74, 75, 76, 77, 78, 80, 81, 82, 83, 84, 87, 88, 89, 90, 91, 92, 93, 95, 96, 97, 98, 105, 106, 108, 111, 113, 115, 117, 123, 128
Kohut, H., 6, 128
Kottler, J. A., 7, 129
Kuhn, T. S., 71, 129
Laurence, Margaret, 35, 129
Letteri, Mark, 11, 42
Locke, John, 31
Longino, H. E., 71, 128
Loseke, D., 60, 129
May, R., 6, 129
McLeod, J., 49
McLeod, John, 16, 19, 31, 42, 60, 131
memory, 29, 34, 35, 36, 40, 42, 43, 53
mental health, 23, 25, 108, 114
Messer, S., 17, 129
Mitchell, S. A., 6, 127
monism, 100, 101
multiplicity, 38, 39, 57, 75, 78, 85, 100, 101, 102, 123
Nietzsche, Friedrich, 1, 3, 24, 25, 26, 33, 35, 36, 37, 38, 39, 54, 56, 73, 79, 81, 83, 90, 100, 102, 104, 105, 107, 115, 125, 126, 127, 128, 129
Ofshe, R., 46, 131

Okruhlik, K., 71, 129
Olkowski, D., 70, 129
Overholser, J. C., 53, 129
Parmenides, 70, 74, 130
Parnet, C., 77, 104, 125
Perls, F., 6, 129
personal identity, 39, 40, 41, 42, 43, 60
phenomenological facts, 99
placebo, 11, 12, 20
Plato, 54, 69, 70, 74, 75, 129, 130
pluralism, 101
Pols, E., 91, 92, 93, 94, 95, 96, 97, 98, 130
postmodern psychotherapy, 23
power, 27, 40, 41, 46, 47, 48, 49, 50, 53, 54, 55, 56, 57, 58, 59, 60, 63, 70, 82, 83, 100, 101, 102, 103, 104, 105, 106, 107, 108, 109, 110, 115, 116, 119, 122, 123
Presocratics, 22, 69
psychoanalysis, 5, 16, 17, 18, 19, 20, 21, 22, 24, 34, 46, 48, 65, 68, 75, 109, 110
Rabinow, P., 57, 126
realism, 3, 9, 37, 57, 78, 87, 88, 89, 90, 91, 92, 93, 94, 95, 98, 99, 100, 104, 105, 106, 107, 108, 109, 110, 111, 113, 115, 116, 117, 122, 123
reconstruction, 2, 3, 5, 9, 21
relativism, 81, 84
representations, 24, 27, 28, 29, 30, 31, 32, 33, 36, 37, 39, 74, 75, 82, 83, 90, 92
repression, 36, 67
Ricoeur, Paul, 19, 22, 130
Rogers, Carl, 6, 16, 130
Rorty, Richard, 19, 22, 130
Rosenthal, D., 46, 51, 130
Rouse, J., 71, 130
Russon, John, 42, 60, 130
Sartre, Jean-Paul, 65, 73, 96, 130
Schafer, Roy, 19, 22, 130
schizoanalysis, 109, 110
Schmideberg, M., 48, 130
Sein, 78, 79

self, the, 3, 5, 6, 7, 8, 9, 10, 11, 12, 13, 14, 15, 16, 17, 20, 23, 24, 25, 26, 30, 31, 33, 34, 35, 36, 37, 39, 40, 41, 42, 43, 44, 45, 46, 47, 50, 52, 55, 57, 58, 59, 60, 61, 63, 64, 65, 66, 67, 68, 81, 83, 84, 97, 99, 108, 113, 114, 115, 118, 119, 122
self-discovery, 3, 5, 7, 52, 119, 122
self-knowledge, 3, 5, 6, 7, 8, 10, 11, 12, 13, 15, 16, 33, 34, 35, 36, 39, 40, 41, 43, 45, 46, 55, 57, 59, 64, 65, 66, 68, 108, 118, 119, 122
serialization, 109
situated realism, 4, 9, 98, 99, 101, 104, 105, 106, 107, 108, 109, 110, 111
social control, 4, 113, 114, 119
Socrates, 54, 74
Spence, Donald, 19, 20, 21, 22, 130
Spinelli, Ernesto, 65, 66, 130
Strupp, H., 6, 10, 48, 49, 51, 52, 130
subjectivity, 1, 2, 3, 15, 25, 26, 28, 32, 33, 34, 35, 36, 37, 38, 39, 40, 41, 42, 43, 47, 64, 65, 69, 71, 72, 74, 78, 79, 81, 83, 87, 98, 103, 105, 108, 109, 111, 113, 115, 123

subjugation, 36, 58, 60
suggestion, 12, 17, 19, 20, 22, 46, 47, 48, 49, 50, 51, 53, 58, 63, 65, 69, 122, 123
suicide, 113, 114
synthesis, 26, 28, 29, 30, 32, 33, 53, 82, 83, 90, 101, 105
Szasz, T., 50, 131
Tally Argument, 19, 20, 21
therapeutic improvement, 6, 8, 13, 68, 108
transcendental subject, 3, 30, 31, 32
truth
    historical t., 20, 21
    narrative t., 21
value-neutrality, 71, 72, 75
Waelder, R., 18, 131
Warren, C. S., 17, 129
Watters, E., 46, 131
Wegrocki, H., 51, 131
will-to-power, 57, 100
Wisdom, John, 19, 22, 131
Wittgenstein, Ludwig, 19, 26, 131
Yalom, Irvin, 5, 6, 13, 34, 131
Yontef, G., 6, 131

VIBS

The **Value Inquiry Book Series** is co-sponsored by:

Adler School of Professional Psychology
American Indian Philosophy Association
American Maritain Association
American Society for Value Inquiry
Association for Process Philosophy of Education
Canadian Society for Philosophical Practice
Center for Bioethics, University of Turku
Center for Professional and Applied Ethics, University of North Carolina at Charlotte
Central European Pragmatist Forum
Centre for Applied Ethics, Hong Kong Baptist University
Centre for Cultural Research, Aarhus University
Centre for Professional Ethics, University of Central Lancashire
Centre for the Study of Philosophy and Religion, University College of Cape Breton
Centro de Estudos em Filosofia Americana, Brazil
College of Education and Allied Professions, Bowling Green State University
College of Liberal Arts, Rochester Institute of Technology
Concerned Philosophers for Peace
Conference of Philosophical Societies
Department of Moral and Social Philosophy, University of Helsinki
Gannon University
Gilson Society
Haitian Studies Association
Ikeda University
Institute of Philosophy of the High Council of Scientific Research, Spain
International Academy of Philosophy of the Principality of Liechtenstein
International Association of Bioethics
International Center for the Arts, Humanities, and Value Inquiry
International Society for Universal Dialogue
Natural Law Society
Philosophical Society of Finland
Philosophy Born of Struggle Association
Philosophy Seminar, University of Mainz
Pragmatism Archive at The Oklahoma State University
R.S. Hartman Institute for Formal and Applied Axiology
Research Institute, Lakeridge Health Corporation
Russian Philosophical Society
Society for Existential Analysis
Society for Iberian and Latin-American Thought
Society for the Philosophic Study of Genocide and the Holocaust
Unit for Research in Cognitive Neuroscience, Autonomous University of Barcelona
Whitehead Research Project
Yves R. Simon Institute

Titles Published

Volumes 1 - 197 see www.rodopi.nl

201.   Carmen R. Lugo-Lugo and Mary K. Bloodsworth-Lugo, Editors, *A New Kind of Containment: "The War on Terror," Race, and Sexuality*. A volume in **Philosophy of Peace**

202.   Amihud Gilead, *Necessity and Truthful Fictions: Panenmentalist Observations*. A volume in **Philosophy and Psychology**

203.   Fernand Vial, *The Unconscious in Philosophy, and French and European Literature: Nineteenth and Early Twentieth Century*. A volume in **Philosophy and Psychology**

204.   Adam C. Scarfe, Editor, *The Adventure of Education: Process Philosophers on Learning, Teaching, and Research*. A volume in **Philosophy of Education**

205.   King-Tak Ip, Editor, *Environmental Ethics: Intercultural Perspectives*. A volume in **Studies in Applied Ethics**

206.   Evgenia Cherkasova, *Dostoevsky and Kant: Dialogues on Ethics*. A volume in **Social Philosophy**

207.   Alexander Kremer and John Ryder, Editors, *Self and Society: Central European Pragmatist Forum*, Volume Four. A volume in **Central European Value Studies**

208.   Terence O'Connell, *Dialogue on Grief and Consolation*. A volume in **Lived Values, Valued Lives**

209.   Craig Hanson, *Thinking about Addiction: Hyperbolic Discounting and Responsible Agency*. A volume in **Social Philosophy**

210.   Gary G. Gallopin, *Beyond Perestroika: Axiology and the New Russian Entrepreneurs*. A volume in **Hartman Institute Axiology Studies**

211.   Tuija Takala, Peter Herissone-Kelly, and Søren Holm, Editors, *Cutting Through the Surface: Philosophical Approaches to Bioethics*. A volume in **Values in Bioethics**

212.   Neena Schwartz: *A Lab of My Own*. A volume in **Lived Values,**

Valued Lives

213. Krzysztof Piotr Skowroński, *Values and Powers: Re-reading the Philosophical Tradition of American Pragmatism*. A volume in **Central European Value Studies**

214. Matti Häyry, Tuija Takala, Peter Herissone-Kelly and Gardar Árnason, Editors, *Arguments and Analysis in Bioethics*. A volume in **Values in Bioethics**

215. Anders Nordgren, *For Our Children: The Ethics of Animal Experimentation in the Age of Genetic Engineering*. A volume in **Values in Bioethics**

216. James R. Watson, Editor, *Metacide: In the Pursuit of Excellence*. A volume in **Holocaust and Genocide Studies**

217. Andrew Fitz-Gibbon, Editor, *Positive Peace: Reflections on Peace Education, Nonviolence, and Social Change*. A volume in **Philosophy of Peace**

218. Christopher Berry Gray, *The Methodology of Maurice Hauriou: Legal, Sociological, Philosophical*. A volume in **Studies in Jurisprudence**

219. Mary K. Bloodsworth-Lugo and Carmen R. Lugo-Lugo, *Containing (Un)American Bodies: Race, Sexuality, and Post-9/11 Constructions of Citizenship*. A volume in **Philosophy of Peace**

220. Roland Faber, Brian G. Henning, Clinton Combs, Editors, *Beyond Metaphysics? Explorations in Alfred North Whitehead's Late Thought*. A volume in **Contemporary Whitehead Studies**

221. John G. McGraw, *Intimacy and Isolation (Intimacy and Aloneness: A Multi-Volume Study in Philosophical Psychology, Volume One)*, A volume in **Philosophy and Psychology**

222. Janice L. Schultz-Aldrich, Introduction and Edition, *"Truth" is a Divine Name, Hitherto Unpublished Papers of Edward A. Synan, 1918-1997*. A volume in **Gilson Studies**

223. Larry A. Hickman, Matthew Caleb Flamm, Krzysztof Piotr Skowroński and Jennifer A. Rea, Editors, *The Continuing Relevance of John*

Dewey: Reflections on Aesthetics, Morality, Science, and Society. A volume in **Central European Value Studies**

224. Hugh P. McDonald, *Creative Actualization: A Meliorist Theory of Values.* A volume in **Studies in Pragmatism and Values**

225. Rob Gildert and Dennis Rothermel, Editors, *Remembrance and Reconciliation.* A volume in **Philosophy of Peace**

226. Leonidas Donskis, Editor, *Niccolò Machiavelli: History, Power, and Virtue.* A volume in **Philosophy, Literature, and Politics**

227. Sanya Osha, *Postethnophilosophy.* A volume in **Social Philosophy**

228. Rosa M. Calcaterra, Editor, *New Perspectives on Pragmatism and Analytic Philosophy.* A volume in **Studies in Pragmatism and Values**

229. Danielle Poe, Editor, *Communities of Peace: Confronting Injustice and Creating Justice.* A volume in **Philosophy of Peace**

230. Thorsten Botz-Bornstein, Editor, *The Philosophy of Viagra: Bioethical Responses to the Viagrification of the Modern World.* A volume in **Philosophy of Sex and Love**

231. Carolyn Swanson, *Reburial of Nonexistents: Reconsidering the Meinong-Russell Debate.* A volume in **Central European Value Studies**

232. Adrianne Leigh McEvoy, Editor, *Sex, Love, and Friendship: Studies of the Society for the Philosophy of Sex and Love: 1993–2003.* A volume in **Histories and Addresses of Philosophical Societies**

233. Amihud Gilead, *The Privacy of the Psychical.* A volume in **Philosophy and Psychology**

234. Paul Kriese and Randall E. Osborne, Editors, *Social Justice, Poverty and Race: Normative and Empirical Points of View.* A volume in **Studies in Jurisprudence**

235. Hakam H. Al-Shawi, *Reconstructing Subjects: A Philosophical Critique of Psychotherapy.* A volume in **Philosophy and Psychology**